Under Mussolini
*Decorative and Propaganda Arts
of the Twenties and Thirties*
from the Wolfson Collection, Genoa

Estorick Collection, London
2 October - 22 December 2002

Under Mussolini
Decorative and Propaganda Arts of the
Twenties and Thirties
from the Wolfson Collection, Genoa

Estorick Collection
39a Canonbury Square
London N1 2AN

Exhibition curated by:
Silvia Barisione, Matteo Fochessati
and Gianni Franzone
The Mitchell Wolfson Jr. Collection -
Fondazione Regionale Cristoforo
Colombo, Genoa

Exhibition organized by:
Roberta Cremoncini and Chris Adams
Estorick Collection, London

Conservation:
Marcello Cambi, Genoa

Photographs:
Mauro Parodi, Genoa; Enrico Polidori,
Genoa; Francesco Saverio Fera, Genoa;
Archivio Alberto Salietti, Genoa

Catalogue translation:
Chris Adams, Kenneth Syme,
Cesare Massimo, Nicholas Cullinan

Acknowledgements:
Aicardi family, Genoa; Susanna Cappai,
The Novecento Corporation, Genoa;
Ugo Carà, Trieste; Gianfranca Carboni,
Genoa; Ferruccio Dilda, Triennale di
Milano; Katia Dabdoub-Hechema, The
Mitchell Wolfson Jr. Private Collection,
Miami; Estorick Collection: Kenneth
Syme, Leonie Taylor; Guido Falconi,
Genoa; Francesco Saverio Fera, Genoa;
Olga Finzi Baldi, Milan; Fondazione
Regionale Cristoforo Colombo, Stefano
Scarpa, Director, Donatella Buongirolami,
Project Coordinator; Alexandra Noble,
former Director of the Estorick Collection;
Gianfranco Pasquino, Professor of
Political Science, University of Bologna
and Johns Hopkins University, Bologna
Centre; Ponis family, Genoa and Rome;
Carmen Ravanelli, Curator, Museo
Internazionale delle Ceramiche, Faenza;
Patrizia Trucco, Library, School of
Architecture, University of Genoa;
The Wolfsonian-FIU, Miami Beach:
Cathy Leff, Director, Richard Miltner,
Exhibition Designer, Kimberly Stillwell
Bergen, Assistant Registrar.

Special thanks to Antonio Tomassini,
Chairman of Euro Catering Foods Ltd.
for his support and to
Music Management (UK) Ltd.

Fondazione Regionale
Cristoforo Colombo, Genoa   Regione Liguria   Comune di Genova   Palazzo Ducale SpA

Estorick Collection
of modern italian art

UNDER MUSSOLINI

Decorative and Propaganda Arts of the Twenties and Thirties
from the Wolfson Collection, Genoa

Silvia Barisione
Matteo Fochessati
Gianni Franzone

Mazzotta

Editing
Giorgio Bigatti

Layout
Roberta Riotti

© 2002 Edizioni Gabriele Mazzotta
Foro Buonaparte 52 - 20121 Milano

ISBN 88-202-1577-2

This exhibition marks a significant moment in the programme of the Estorick Collection: it is in fact the first time that the entire building has been dedicated to a project with no permanent collection on display. We decided to take up the challenge and lend over 100 works from the permanent collection, including the most important masterpieces, to Genoa in an exchange with the Wolfson Collection. The Estorick Collection will be on show for the first time since its opening nearly five years ago at Genoa's Palazzo Ducale, offering a unique opportunity for it to be seen in a completely different environment.

Under Mussolini: Decorative and Propaganda Arts of the Twenties and Thirties documents two decades of Italian art from Mussolini's rise to power to his fall in 1943. The selection of works chosen from the large and fascinating Wolfson Collection is based around various historical events which took place during the Fascist era and aims to illustrate how, despite the tragedy of Fascism, artists continued to produce interesting and beautiful works of art in many different and contrasting styles, which can be appreciated above and beyond their political dimensions. We believe it is important to analyse every aspect of a phenomenon in order to be able to understand the errors of such a period and to prevent history repeating itself. This fascinating journey through the applied arts of the Twenties and Thirties will be a revelation to our public, who will be able to appreciate for the first time the diversity and richness of Italian art in this period.

I would like to thank the exhibition curators, Silvia Barisione, Matteo Fochessati and Gianni Franzone, with whom we have worked extremely well over the past two years; and Professor Gianfranco Pasquino, who so enthusiastically accepted my idea of writing an historical introduction to the period for our catalogue that puts the entire exhibition in a proper context. I would also like to thank Gabriele Mazzotta for believing in the project and producing such a wonderful catalogue for us. Naturally, my thanks also go to Micky Wolfson, firstly for having put together such a fantastic collection and also for his enthusiasm in promoting this project. My thanks also go to the Fondazione Regionale Cristoforo Colombo, which administers the Wolfson Collection, and its President, Franco Ragazzi. Finally, I would like to mention my staff and everybody who has helped throughout the past months to organize and prepare every stage of this exhibition.

Roberta Cremoncini
Director, Estorick Collection

The exhibition *Under Mussolini: Decorative and Propaganda Arts of the Twenties and Thirties*, and its accompanying catalogue, aims to offer the British public a broad cross-section of Italian art from the Fascist era.
As is well known, both the artistic production of the *ventennio* – the two decades of Fascist rule – and the aesthetic guidelines that were its foundation, do not appear to have been characterized by a unity and homogeneity of sources of inspiration and expressive styles. The different spirits of the regime saw, therefore, their materialization in the artistic form that found inspiration in the exaltation of military power or in the cult of the *Duce*, rather than in the social policies of the regime and post-war discontent. At the same time, artistic styles were evolving in radical directions.
The curators of the exhibition have faithfully conveyed this variety which represents the true "richness" of "Fascist" art.
The complexity of this panorama is also examined in the context of the evolution of the regime over time: from the atmosphere which followed the March on Rome and the elections of 1924, to the years of the consolidation of power and consensus that reached a climax in the construction of the empire, and finally to the outbreak of the Second World War and the establishment of the Italian Social Republic.
The visitor to the exhibition and the reader of this catalogue will find paintings, sculptures and architectural projects for buildings required by the regime. In this context one should point out that in Genoa and Liguria there were a number of significant projects. A place of importance is given to the exhibitions and trade fairs that Fascism organized to great communicatory and evocative effect.
This variety of expressive forms is nowhere more apparent than in the so-called minor arts, and the exhibition contains examples of works in styles ranging from Art Déco to the Novecento and Rationalism.
It is a source of great pride that all of this material belongs to that part of the Wolfson Collection entrusted by its owner – in concert with the Ligurian Regional Council – to the Fondazione Regionale Cristoforo Colombo, and which represents the feather in its cap.
This exhibition, once more, underscores the historical links that bind Liguria and Great Britain and aims to reveal to the British public the richness of our region's cultural patrimony.

Sandro Biasotti
President, Ligurian Regional Council

It gives me great pleasure to introduce this important new cultural initiative realized by the Mitchell Wolfson Jr. Collection through a collaboration between it and the City of Genoa, the Fondazione Regionale Cristoforo Colombo, the Ligurian Regional Council and the Estorick Collection of London.

The Wolfson Collection's exhibition, *Under Mussolini: Decorative and Propaganda Arts of the Twenties and Thirties*, hosted by the Estorick Collection of Modern Italian Art, is mirrored by a contemporaneous exhibition in Genoa, at Palazzo Ducale, of masterpieces from the Estorick Collection.

This represents a cultural exchange of the highest level whose value I am especially aware of as Mayor of Genoa – 2004 European City of Culture.

The positive result of the collaboration between civic bodies and institutions in supporting and promoting the Wolfson Collection, from which this project has originated, confirms the intentions of this administration, directed at fostering a synergy between different entities so as to reach common objectives that are in the interests of the city.

I would like to take this opportunity to stress the high esteem in which the City of Genoa holds the cultural activity of the Mitchell Wolfson Jr. Collection. The selection of works for this exhibition is of a very high quality and is intended to represent a broad spectrum of the figurative and decorative arts in Italy during the period that witnessed the emergence, establishment and collapse of Fascism. It offers an opportunity for the British public to appraise the evolution of aesthetics in one of the most difficult periods in my country's history.

On the other hand, the exhibition of Italian art hosted at the same time in Genoa's Palazzo Ducale – the most high-profile venue in the city for cultural events – offers visitors the opportunity to see, at first-hand, masterpieces by artists such as Morandi, Guttuso, Marini and Manzù, drawn from the historic period between 1890 and 1950.

The Genoese community considers 2004, and the role which the city has been called upon to play in the course of that year, to be an unmissable occasion for Genoa to "re-launch" itself on the international stage, and an extraordinary opportunity to promote our city's impressive artistic and cultural patrimony, which still awaits due recognition.

For these reasons, the project of the Mitchell Wolfson Jr. and Estorick Collections represents a new pearl to be added to the already precious string of events which will be taking place in the lead up to 2004.

In the name of the city of Genoa I therefore wish to extend my heartfelt thanks to all those who have made this initiative possible.

Giuseppe Pericu
Mayor of Genoa

Following the exhibitions *La Visione del Prisma* in Parma – a title adapted from one of Ferruccio Ferrazzi's most significant paintings – and *Parole e Immagini Futuriste*, shown in New York and San Francisco, the Wolfson Collection now travels to London's Estorick Collection, an institution devoted to twentieth century Italian artistic culture.
Since 1999 the Fondazione Regionale Cristoforo Colombo has administered the collection of Mitchell Wolfson Jr. – a duty with which it was entrusted, and in which it is supported, by the Ligurian Regional Council and the City of Genoa. The fruit of many years of passionate, informed research, the Collection was presented to the people of Liguria in an act of selfless generosity.
For the Fondazione Colombo this exhibition is a source of great pride and satisfaction – as is the realization of an exchange which today sees the Estorick Collection displayed in Genoa's Palazzo Ducale, the ancient Doges' Palace of the Genoese Republic and today a venue for great artistic and cultural events, as well as the home of the Fondazione Colombo itself.
I shall leave it to the historians to introduce the content of the present exhibition, and allow the works to speak for themselves – works of art and propaganda, and objects forming part of the fabric of the everyday life of an era which lasted little more than twenty years. This era – known in Italy as the *ventennio*, during which the country was "under Mussolini" – witnessed a generation pass from exultation over victory in the First World War, and widespread endorsement of an authoritarian regime, to the anguish produced by a terrible conflict that devastated cities and lacerated the conscience of the Italian people. It is not, however, the aim of this exhibition to pass judgement on that period: the works discovered, conserved and studied by Mitchell Wolfson Jr. revisit history and enable us to better understand the past so as to better construct the future.

Franco Ragazzi
Chairman, Fondazione Regionale Cristoforo Colombo

The figure of the art collector has always been a source of interest, curiosity and admiration for me. It has been a long-held ambition of mine to organize a wide-ranging programme of exhibitions analysing the key role played by the collector: art seen through the eyes of those who buy it, conserve it and for whom it is an all-consuming passion.

This extraordinary exchange between the Estorick and Wolfson Collections – which offers Genoa and London the opportunity to swap two very fine exhibitions that themselves represent true aesthetic adventures having strong cultural reverberations – both realizes and exceeds my aspiration, since it not only allows the presentation of works of art, but also the opportunity of evaluating two approaches to the art of collecting (for in the case of Eric Estorick and Mitchell Wolfson Jr. one may truly speak of "collecting as art"). It is an astonishing fact that the interest of both men lay in Italian art of the same era – that is, the late nineteenth and early twentieth centuries – and their great legacy has been that of allowing us to develop deeper and more informed intellectual and emotional responses to the cultural achievements of this period.

Arnaldo Bagnasco
Chairman, Palazzo Ducale SpA

Contents

13 Forward
Silvia Barisione, Matteo Fochessati, Gianni Franzone

15 Under Mussolini
Gianfranco Pasquino

21 The Politics of Persuasion: Art and Propaganda under Fascism
Matteo Fochessati

29 Santagata and Salietti: Two Examples of Mural Painting from the Wolfson Collection between the "Fascistization" of Italy and the Collapse of the Regime
Franco Ragazzi

37 The Decorative Arts in Italy from the Monza "Biennale" to the Milan "Triennale"
Silvia Barisione

47 The Demographic Colonization of Libya: Propaganda, Art and Architecture
Gianni Franzone

55 Catalogue

105 List of Works

Forward

Since the Wolfson Collection – dedicated to art of the period between 1885 and 1945 – is primarily concerned with historical and political imagery and the evolution of the applied arts, this exhibition aims to document the two decades of Fascist rule through a selection of different media: painting, sculpture, graphic design, photography, furnishings, ceramics and glassware.
Taking as its starting point a number of important historical focal points – the March on Rome of 1922, the national elections of 1924, the Lateran Pacts of 1929 and the colonial venture of the 1930s – the exhibition has been designed to provide an evocative analysis of the events and tastes of the era. It investigates some of the most significant elements of the regime's propaganda drive, such as the so-called "Battle for Grain," the attempts to evoke Augustan *romanità*, the iconography of Mussolini-related imagery and the organization of youth within the structure of the *Balilla* association.
If in the sphere of the figurative arts the exhibition documents the self-celebration of the regime – including significant examples of decorative cycles conceived for public buildings – then it also highlights how Fascist iconography, although frequently incorporated into the design of everyday objects, exerted only a minimal influence upon the development of the decorative arts in Italy at this time, and how Italian designers – taking their inspiration from vernacular traditions – contributed to the renovation of the applied arts throughout Europe.

Silvia Barisione, Matteo Fochessati, Gianni Franzone

Marcello Dudovich, *Roman Salute*, 1925
(cat. no. 7)

Under Mussolini

Gianfranco Pasquino

Paolo Troubetzkoy, *Benito Mussolini*, 1926 (cat. no. 11)

The aftermath of the First World War found the Italian political, institutional and social systems in a state of distress. In practice, Italy found herself on the side of those who had won the war, but the price to be paid for this victory was very high indeed. Economically, the country had depleted many of her not very plentiful resources. Politically, the rift between those who had pushed for entry into the war and those who had opposed it ran very deep. Socially, many tensions were arising among those young and middle-aged men who had fought in the war, and whose family life had been disrupted by it, and those who had succeeded in avoiding the draft. Tensions ran especially high among the veterans, many of them non-commissioned officers of middle class or of petty bourgeois origins, who felt abandoned, even scorned in some cases, and could not find a decent job. The dislocations caused by the war and the impact of the Russian Revolution also seemed to galvanize several sectors of the working class led by Socialist, and later also by Communist organizers who had themselves opposed the war.

Most, though not all, of these tensions were translated into a battle for the ballots of Italian voters. For the 1919 elections two major changes occurred simultaneously: an expansion of the suffrage and the introduction of proportional representation. The party representing the relative majority of voters up to this point, the Liberal Party led by Giovanni Giolitti, had to face competition from two well-organized parties: the traditional Socialist Party, that had already been in existence for almost twenty years, but was to suffer the Communist split in 1921, and the Popular Party, recently founded by a priest, Don Luigi Sturzo, and rapidly expanding thanks to the wide network of Catholic associations. Unfortunately for themselves and, as it transpired, for Italian democracy, the loose liberal élites had failed in their historic task of constructing a vehicle, similar to other conservative parties in Western Europe, for the political representation of the interests of the bourgeoisie. The emerging Fascist movement, led by the former Socialist journalist Benito Mussolini, who had vehemently supported the war, capitalized on the discontent of the veterans and on what was aptly called "status panic": that is, the fear of the middle classes of succumbing to a well-organized and militant industrial working class. As they were subsequently to do in several other European countries, Italian Fascists resorted to a series of prolonged violent activities. Again, as in these other countries, the Italian State and its apparatuses were neither sufficiently well equipped nor particularly willing to repress the disorder caused by middle class activists, supported in different areas

by northern industrialists and by Po Valley landowners who wanted to tame the industrial working class and prevent the organization of landless peasants and the redistribution of property. Almost ignored by the police and the prefects, the threat posed by the Fascists was either underestimated by the moderate politicians, by the Monarchy and by the forces of order, or was considered a good opportunity to disband and subdue the working class and its political leaders.
The famous March on Rome organized by Mussolini on 28 October 1922 was an almost farcical event, though one with tragic consequences. It occurred when the occupation of northern factories (such as Fiat in Turin) by industrial workers had already been defeated, as had the battle for property by landless rural workers. Mussolini arrived in Rome by train and, though the leader of a minor party counting only thirty-five deputies in parliament, was immediately appointed head of the Italian government by King Victor Emmanuel III. In effect the State, its authorities and its prefects had surrendered to Fascist violence. Incidentally, this is the reason why the male descendants of the royal family of Savoy were banned from returning to Italy after the enactment of the Republican Constitution in 1948 (the ban was lifted by the present government in July 2002). The leader of the Fascists started to persecute and, whenever necessary, kill his enemies, having figures such as Piero Gobetti and Giovanni Amendola beaten to death. The kidnapping and assassination of the outspoken Socialist Giacomo Matteotti marked the institution of the Fascist regime. In an infamous speech of January 1925 Mussolini claimed full responsibility for this event, but there was no opposition capable of calling for his resignation. The court and the forces around the King even condoned his brutal act. Mussolini arrogantly and happily accepted the label of "totalitarian" that his anti-Fascist liberal opponents used to characterize the regime he was attempting to create. Originally, however, Fascism had possessed an anti-capitalist, secular, almost revolutionary vision and Mussolini had declared himself a republican. Indeed, several "Fascists of the first hour" continued to cherish expectations of a profound transformation of the Italian political and socio-economic system. The cudgel that symbolized early Fascism was quickly shelved, though never spared when deemed necessary. It was replaced by a formal outfit, a double-breasted suit. However, Mussolini the *Duce* often returned to the original black shirt duly worn by his supporters, or *camerati*, and imposed upon all civil servants, bureaucrats and school teachers.
Before "normalizing" his rule and creating what ended up constituting the Fascist regime, however, Mussolini had vainly tried to pursue the totalitarian path, to construct a strong party and a strong State. However, he chose not to challenge the Monarchy. Nor was he ever capable of "Fascistizing," or acquiring full control over, the armed forces (which remained loyal to the King) or the bureaucracy (which remained passive, but never became citizen-friendly). He came to terms with the very powerful Catholic Church, first signing the Lateran Pacts in 1929 then, in 1931, drafting a Concordat which granted the Church a relatively free hand in the fields of education (schools at all levels) and medical care (hospitals, nursery homes), but which barred it from political activities. More preoccupied by the Bolshevik menace, Pope Pius XI referred to Mussolini as the "Man of Providence," thus legitimizing his rule in the eyes of the traditionally Catholic masses. By the mid-1930s, the nature of the Fascist regime had become clear: whilst authoritarian it could no longer aspire to become totalitarian, as German National Socialism was.
The National Fascist Party (PNF) never became so powerful and all-pervasive as the Nazi Party. Never a dominant organization, the PNF had to share power with the Monarchy and in selected areas with the industrialists, the landowners, the Church, the armed forces and the bureaucrats. The secretary of the party never

Guido Galletti, *Boy Throwing a Stone (Balilla)*, 1931
(cat. no. 76)

Antonio (Tony) Lucarda, *Balilla Drummer-Boy*, 1934
(cat. no. 77)

Bot (Oswaldo Barbieri Terribile), *Opera Balilla Grade I Diploma*, 1934 (cat. no. 78)

Luccio (Carlo Bolognesi) *Italian Products*, c. 1922 (cat. no. 91)

became an especially important political authority. Certainly, *primus inter pares*, the *Duce* of Italian Fascism had to bargain with several powerful organizations and to settle tensions and quarrels. Fascism never renounced violence, though by the mid-1930s the internal opposition was limited to a few activities by the Communists, who badly misjudged the nature of Fascism, and to exemplary actions by *Giustizia e Libertà*. The bourgeois and intellectual leaders of this organization, such as Ernesto Rossi and Vittorio Foa, and of the Italian Communist Party, such as Altiero Spinelli, were either sent to prison or sentenced to confinement for many years. Hundreds of anti-Fascists were obliged to go into exile and many (among them Leo Valiani, mentioned in the famous book by Arthur Koestler) decided to fight in the International Brigades during the Spanish Civil War (1936-39). The dispersal of the Italian anti-Fascists was very diversified: the Communist leader Palmiro Togliatti found refuge in Moscow, Don Luigi Sturzo in New York, the famous historian Gaetano Salvemini went to Harvard and the brothers Carlo and Nello Rosselli were killed in 1937 in France by a joint action of the Fascist secret police and a right-wing French group. By that time, Mussolini had reached his apex in terms of popularity, recognition and personal power.

Following the conquest of Ethiopia, the Italian King acquired the title of Emperor (1935) and the existence of an Italian empire seemed to satisfy many an ambition and to prove that small Italy (*l'Italietta*) had become a great power like her alleged predecessor the Roman Empire, whose many symbols were resuscitated by Fascism. The regime had certainly acquired popular acceptance, but can one say, as Renzo De Felice wrote, that Mussolini also enjoyed the consensus of the majority of Italians? Certainly, if there was consensus for Fascist rule its amount and extent could by no means be measured. Throughout most of Italy, largely a rural country made up of a myriad of small towns at the time, political consensus was imposed upon the citizens by local authorities, the national government appointed mayor, or *podestà*, the chief of police, the barrister, the priest – in sum, the "notables" – and by the mechanisms of social control over any kind of dissent and non-conformism that always exist in small communities. Whenever necessary, or just for the fun of it, the bosses of local Fascist squads, termed *ras*, provided some intimidation and beating, or obliged those who were not conforming to drink massive doses of castor oil. In any case, it was at the most a *passive* consensus dictated by the desire of many Italians and their families to lead a quiet life (although there was almost always a bizarre "uncle" or relative who would object to Fascism). If there was consensus it was certainly not channelled by the few existing self-defined Fascist intellectuals, none of whom was particularly innovative or capable of reaching an international audience. What is considered the cultural monument of Fascism, the *Enciclopedia Treccani*, was directed and edited by a famous philosopher, Giovanni Gentile – a disciple of Croce's, who can in fact be considered probably the only "Fascist intellectual" worth this title. By no means the exclusive product of Fascist painters, sculptors, architects or writers, Futurism continued to flourish under Fascism – but it was tolerated rather than celebrated by Fascist leaders, who had a much more traditional view of the arts and their role in society.

The one who was not satisfied and who by temperament could certainly not lead a quiet life was Mussolini himself. He was envious of the successes and power of Adolf Hitler (perhaps the best characterization of the relationship between the two men can be found in Charlie Chaplin's movie *The Great Dictator*). When the Second World War arrived Mussolini did not want to miss the opportunity to act and, though ill-prepared, decided to launch Italy into the conflict in the mistaken belief that it was going to be short, painless and profitable. By mid-1943 it was clear even to the Fascists that Italy was going to be overwhelmed by the consequences of a war that could not be won. On 25 July 1943, the Fascist Grand Council outvoted Mussolini and immediately thereafter the King, amidst joyful popular manifestations, dismissed him. The entire authoritarian configuration collapsed, but Mussolini did not give up. Buttressed by the Germans, in what the English historian Frederick W. Deakin called "the brutal friendship," Mussolini revived early Fascism: ruthless, anti-capitalist and, above all, anti-monarchist. His Italian Social Republic recruited the most violent youngsters and drafted all those who could not escape. It fought a rearguard battle against those Italians who were taking up arms to overthrow the occupying Nazi forces. The Italian Social Republic precipitated a civil war and furiously engaged in it. The war ended in April 1945 when Italy was liberated by resistance fighters and the Allies. Apprehended by the partisans, Mussolini and his mistress were killed and strung up in a square in Milan.

A regime that had been born out of the unscrupulous and violent exploitation of the consequences of World War One ended as it had begun: in war, in destruction, in disarray. If, as some nostalgists are fond of putting it, Fascism was the almost inevitable product of a necessary modernization, only a limited amount of uneven modernization had been produced. Many Italians continued to migrate abroad, to the USA and Latin America. Most of those who remained in Italy did not see their living conditions improved in terms of jobs, education or health. Whatever had been modernized was largely destroyed by the war after which "victorious" Italy (having joined the camp of the Allies after September 1943) was engulfed in the necessary process of painful reconstruction. Only in the republican and democratic framework that was created after World War Two, in fact, could Italy show her ability to change, to improve, to become the sixth industrial power in the world.

It would be a serious mistake to believe, as the famous Italian philosopher Benedetto Croce said, that Fascism was just an interlude in a peaceful trajectory of the Italian political system and its emerging democracy, and that Mussolini was nothing but its mastermind. On the contrary, Fascism was a true Italian product: the consequence of an imperfect social and cultural modernization, of a frail and limited democracy and of the behaviour of fearful, lazy, backward industrial and political élites and their religious counterparts. In sum, exactly as the liberal anti-Fascists had immediately observed, Fascism was the autobiography of a nation. It has taken a while to write a new and not yet fully satisfactory biography.

Giorgio Matteo Aicardi, *Duce. Studies for the fresco on a building façade in Busalla (Genoa) on the occasion of the visit of Mussolini to Genoa, May 1938*, 1938
(cat. no. 82)

The Politics of Persuasion: Art and Propaganda under Fascism

Matteo Fochessati

The Duce in Genoa, May XVI, 1938
Photo Cresta

For me the masses are nothing other than a flock of sheep until they are organized. I am not completely against them. I only deny that they can govern themselves by themselves... This is what Fascism intends to do to the masses: organize a collective life, a common life, so as to work and fight in a hierarchy without flocks... Only faith moves mountains... not reason. This is an instrument, but can never be used as the principal force in motivating the masses, today less than ever before. People today have less time to think. The disposition of modern man to believe is incredible. When I feel the masses in my hands, as it were, or when I mix myself with them then I feel a part of them. And yet at the same time I feel a little disgusted about them... Does not the sculptor perhaps smash the marble out of rage when it does not conform precisely to his original vision? Everything depends on this, on dominating the masses like an artist.

(Benito Mussolini, in Emilio Ludwig [ed.], *Colloqui con Mussolini*, Milan, 1932, pp. 119-25)

Benito Mussolini perceived a strong analogy between political action and artistic practice, as was made clear during his speech at the inauguration of the *Prima Mostra del Novecento Italiano* at the Palazzo della Permanente, Milan, on 15 February 1926.[1] And yet, notwithstanding his will to endow the regime with a new artistic patrimony, to create – in his own words – "a new art for our times, a Fascist art,"[2] the material he intended to shape, through a systematic work of aestheticizing politics, was the Italian people. Lack of space prevents us from discussing in detail the complexities of the relationship between art and power in Mussolini's Italy. Instead, I intend to analyse the nature of the interaction between the visual arts and Fascist propaganda, identifying the principal thematic contents and the emergent stylistic tendencies. We are not concerned, therefore, with examining the problematic aspects of a Fascist art that even from a stylistic point of view did not present the same uniformity as that of Nazism, and which by virtue of its complexity has been the object of important studies during recent years, even in the form of major international exhibitions.[3] It seems more appropriate – given the specific context of this exhibition – to explore what image of Fascist Italy was promoted by the large contemporary exhibitions organized by the regime and by the public art of monumental decoration in the field of mural painting, and what methods the propaganda of the regime employed in this respect, in support of a unifying politics and of a sought-after international recognition.

---

[1] See P. Barocchi, *Storia moderna dell'arte in Italia: Dal Novecento ai dibattiti sulla figura e sul monumentale 1925-1945*, vol. III, Turin, 1990, pp. 9-12.
[2] From Mussolini's speech at the Accademia di Belle Arti in Perugia on 5 October 1926, in V. Araldi, *Mussolini parla: Un venticinquennio di storia attraverso la parola del Duce*, Rome, 1943, p. 162.
[3] See *Art and Power: Europe Under the Dictators 1930-45*, Hayward Gallery, London, 1995; J. Tabor, *Kunst und Diktatur: Architektur, Bildhauerei und Malerei in Österreich, Deutschland, Italien und der Sowjetunion 1922-1956*, Künstlerhaus, Vienna, 1994.

Filiberto Scarpelli, *Italy Abroad*, 1924
(cat. no. 9)

Filiberto Scarpelli, *The Lira*, 1924
(cat. no. 10)

Nico Edel, *Vercelli and its Province from Romanità to Fascism*, 1939 (cat. no. 30)

In wishing to focus this use of politics as propaganda with respect to the field of the visual arts, it will, however, be necessary to briefly summarize the issues associated with the cultural administration of Fascism. The question of an art of the State was in fact raised by Mussolini himself on the occasion of his aforementioned speech at the *Prima Mostra del Novecento Italiano*, but also by Giuseppe Bottai on the occasion of his inquest into Fascist art, which was published in his review *Critica Fascista*.[4] In reality – and in marked contrast to the situation in Germany, where an art of the State was constructed from the precise guidelines of a severe and rigid political culture which led to a ferocious repression of the phenomenon of so-called "degenerate art" – in Italy the Fascist government set about the organization and tutelage of artists in the context of a corporative State, operating a control on individualism and stifling voices of opposition in the structure of the unions. The regimentation of the various expressive tendencies which coexisted under Fascism, often confronting one another – as in the case of the cultural bipolarity represented by Bottai and Roberto Farinacci – was sustained by the reinforcement of exhibition institutions such as the Venice *Biennale* or the Milan *Triennale*, or else by the creation of new bodies, such as the *Quadriennale* of Rome, but above all by the widespread organization of syndicate shows at a local and regional level.[5] Thus, the Fascist regime did not intervene directly in matters of aesthetics, but rather limited itself to preparing a socialization of the artistic product in the context of the organizational structure of the corporative State. This model of political control, in its intention of definitively abolishing the juridical form of the Liberal State and its entire process of democratic development, anticipated a global project of social and economic reorganization which, in essence, foresaw the personal contribution of each individual and every professional class to the productivity and richness of the nation. The link between citizen and State was thus to be considered indissoluble, as such a union was founded on work, understood as a social necessity for the entire population, and on the ethical and political co-responsibility of the individual to the productive process of the collective.

Returning, therefore, to analyse the initiatives prepared by the regime in the attempt to create that "fabric of consensus"[6] which produced itself, as one has seen, in a double action towards the exterior and the interior, one notes how, beyond the different stylistic solutions adopted – including returns to classical tradition and avant-garde experimentation – there emerge a number of recurrent themes, often related to the aesthetic choices of the products of this complex propagandistic organization.

Firstly, Fascism prepares, by means of a subjective re-reading of historical events, its own political legitimization which, depending on the situation, bases itself on the manipulated interpretation of the most recent news or on the projection into the more distant past of its own aspirations for the future. Secondly, especially in the sphere of ephemeral events that were public in character such as exhibitions, fairs, or demonstrations there emerged the desire to document the political affirmation of the regime through testaments to its supremacy in the field of public works and, above all, its programmatic scheme for the transformation of everyday life for the Italians.

The political imagery promoted by Mussolini's dictatorship did not in fact limit itself to a rigid and tight internal control via messages aimed at reassuring the population while increasing its sense of pride, but tended to transform the reality of the entire nation under the mark of Mussolini, who not by coincidence, as early as 1926 on the occasion of a speech made at Reggio Emilia had stated: "Comrades, in ten years time Italy will be unrecognizable! We will have transformed her, we will have made her into another land, from the mountains that we will

[4] G. Bottai, "Resultanze dell'inchiesta sull'arte fascista", in *Critica Fascista*, V, no. 4, 15 February 1927.
[5] A leading figure in the Fascist regime, Giuseppe Bottai played a role of the utmost importance in the cultural life of the Fascist era through his political and legislative position, in addition to his promotional activity carried on through the journals founded and directed by him (*Critica Fascista*, *Le Arti* and *Primato*). Farinacci, one of the most lively supporters of the Racial Laws, founded and directed the newspaper *Il Regime Fascista* (1926-45) and instituted the *Premio Cremona*, inspired by the cultural politics of Nazism, which was first held in 1939.
[6] P.V. Cannistraro, *La fabbrica del consenso*, Bari, 1975.

have covered in their necessary green foliage, to the fields that we will have reclaimed, to the railways that we will have increased, to the ports that we will have equipped."⁷

If, therefore, as declared by Forges Davanzati, presenter of the radio show *Chronicles of the Regime* in the 4 February 1935 transmission "the first work of art of the Regime is the Regime itself," it appears to be obvious that the primary objective of the cultural politics of Fascism was that of offering to a wider audience a new image of the nation that linked the identity of the citizens to the State.

It is not by chance that this type of message lost validity after 1943, in the years of the Italian Social Republic, in a time when propaganda no longer presented itself as a support to a consolidated political government, but rather as a search for a new consensus projected onto visionary and apocalyptic fears *vis-à-vis* the impending disaster: a halo of tragic fatality that pervaded, in particular, the poster designing of Gino Boccasile, who ever since the painful allegorical portrayal of the betrayal of 25 July was the artist who most closely chronicled the fall of Mussolini's dictatorship (cat. no. 80).

In the years when the regime's popularity was at its peak, Fascist propaganda focused instead on the organization of large expositions that, in contrast to the artistic exhibitions that were aimed at a more specialist public, transformed themselves into media events that involved large crowds of visitors. Such exhibitions, which were modelled on international fairs, presented themselves as historical celebrations of Fascism and of its great technological, industrial and agricultural works. A more innovative approach was found in these than in the mural paintings that were commissioned for the decoration of public edifices. In terms of iconography and style a more classical approach was adapted in consideration of their permanence and desired durability.

Exceptions to this, however, are the sculptural murals executed by the Futurists and the experience of Mario Sironi, the main protagonist of the new artistic period of the Novecento movement in the 1930s.⁸ Considering the number of public works and exhibitions that characterized the cultural politics and patronage of the Fascist regime we will have to limit ourselves to a few significant examples which are directly relevant to the current exhibition and on which information is conserved in the extensive documentation on the period at the Wolfson Collection in Genoa. A paradigmatic model for all subsequent exhibitions arranged by the Fascist regime was the *Mostra della Rivoluzione Fascista*, held in Rome's Palazzo delle Esposizioni in 1932 to celebrate the tenth anniversary of the March on Rome,⁹ intended as a documentary and popular show on the history of the seizing of power by the Fascists and their subsequent political affirmation. The exhibition was characterized by a strongly innovative stylistic selection from the point of view of expressive solutions, beginning with the design of Mario De Renzi and Adalberto Libera for the façade of the nineteenth century building that was covered by a large red cube upon which four *fasces* of sheet metal were made to stand out, resting on a cantilevered roof with the title of the exhibition in large characters painted with nitrocellulose. Inside, each room was curated by an historian for the documentary element and by an artist for the pictorial element. Along the exhibition itinerary – with rooms designed by the likes of Sironi, Achille Funi, Enrico Prampolini, Gerardo Dottori, Marcello Nizzoli and Giuseppe Terragni – the reconstruction of the principal Italian historical events from 1914 to 1922 strongly emphasized the nation's participation in the conflict as a preliminary event in the rise of the regime and the theme of the martyrs that Fascism consecrated during the taking of power. The symbolic space of this "mythicizing" of the beginnings of Fascism were represented by Adalberto Libera and Antonio Valente in a sanctuary to the martyrs. Planned as a sacred space, this circular room

A. Motti, *Caius Iulius Caesar Octavianus Augustus A.R. DCLXXXXI A.D. MCMXXVII - XV E.F.*, 1937

Duilio Cambellotti, *Study for decorations in the Palazzo dell'Acquedotto Pugliese in Bari*, 1931

⁷ In V. Araldi, *op. cit.*, p. 164.
⁸ On Sironi and Italian mural painting see V. Fagone, G. Ginex, T. Sparagni (eds), *Muri ai pittori: Pittura murale e decorazione in Italia 1930-1950*, Museo della Permanente, Milan, 1999, and in particular about the Futurist experience M. Fochessati, "La plastica murale: Teorie ed esperienze", pp. 71-82.
⁹ The Wolfson Collection has an archive of photographic documentation about the *Mostra della Rivoluzione Fascista*, together with guides, catalogues and other original documents.

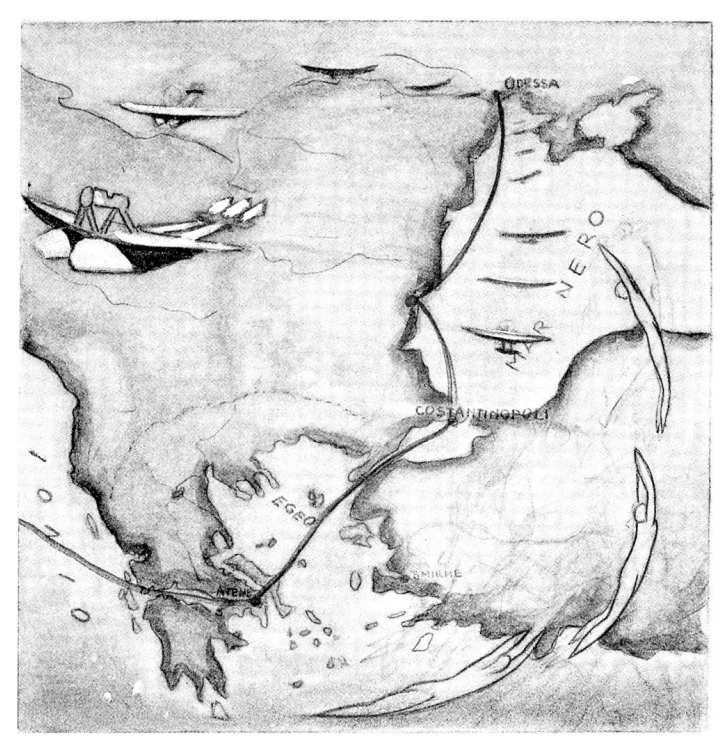

Italo Balbo's Crossing. Studies for decorations in the Ministry of Aeronautics in Rome, c. 1931
(cat. no. 40)

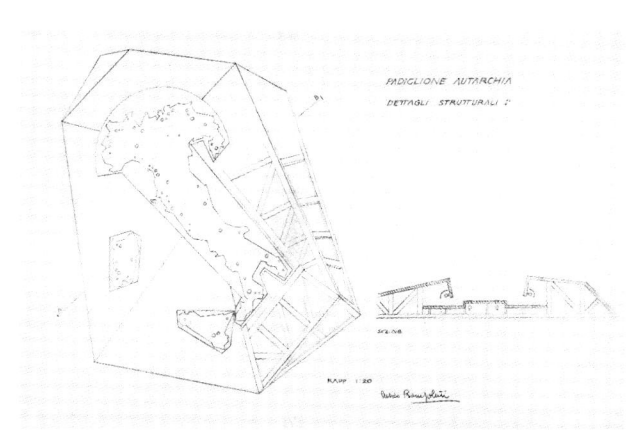

Enrico Prampolini, *Autarchy Pavilion, structural details I*, 1939

Michele Busiri Vici, *Italian Pavilion. New York World's Fair*, 1939

with "Present!" inscribed obsessively on its walls, encouraged the visitor to linger in reflecting on the supreme sacrifice of those that were identified as incarnations of extreme loyalty to the country, to the party and the *Duce*. Continuing onto the floor above, with the section dedicated to the exploits of the regime, the first part of the exhibition, focusing on the historical legitimization of recent events, represented the heart of the exhibition space, where one reflected symbolically upon the image of Mussolini.

In a plastic synthesis by Sironi in Room P, the *Duce* was symbolized as a Roman sword severing a heavy chain, finally cutting the too numerous knots of Gordius that for too long had bridled Italian life. It is not by accident that analogous symbols are employed by Ernesto Thayaht in his painting *The Great Helmsman* of 1939 (cat. no. 119), in which Mussolini, transfigured into a sort of robot devoid of any physiognomic characteristics, breaks the chains imposed by Italy's enemies. The exhibition juxtaposed the emblematic figure of Mussolini with the anonymous depiction of the masses, charged with the aesthetic of violence that Fascism derived from Futurism's cult of youth, and upon whom the *Duce* had imposed the rule to "live dangerously." Beyond the evocation of the specific themes of their poetry, the Futurists claimed responsibility for the stylistic display of the exhibition which consisted largely of photography in the form of photomontages, and of publicity style graphics and lettering. It was in such details that it resembled El Lissitsky's efforts in the Soviet Pavilion at the *International Press Exhibition* of Cologne in 1928.[10] More in keeping with the purposes of propaganda was the critical reception given to the event by Margherita Sarfatti, the theorist of the Novecento movement, who in an article that appeared in January 1933 in the review entitled *Architettura*, underlined the sacred and mystical aspects of this show "conceived as a cathedral whose walls speak."[11]

In this work of counterfeit history the definitive passage from recent events to more remote periods took place with the *Mostra Augustea della Romanità*, held at the same venue in 1937, the two thousandth anniversary of Emperor Augustus's birth and a date intended to symbolically link the splendour of imperial Rome and the greatness of Fascist Rome.[12] The variants of iconography that illustrated this classical Roman spirit, evoked in celebration of the glory of the Fascist regime, were many, but often, as in the case of the bas-reliefs by Antonio Maraini for the *Arengario* in Piazza della Vittoria by Marcello Piacentini, the wax model of which is in the Wolfson Collection, it was the lictor's *fasces* that visually embodied the historical continuity between the two eras.[13]

In the meantime, another means of recapturing past greatness was pursued in the form of the *V Triennale* of Milan in 1933 which, under the direction of Sironi, inaugurated the new Palazzo dell'Arte of Giovanni Muzio with murals in the chamber of ceremonies executed by some of the most renowned Italian artists of the day, such as Massimo Campigli, Achille Funi, Gino Severini, Giorgio de Chirico, Carlo Carrà and Corrado Cagli.

Sironi, who in 1932 had already published an article on mural painting, in which he urged a return to the integration between the arts in the context of "new problems of space, form and expression, of lyrical, epic and dramatic content," was the main contributor to the *Manifesto della Pittura murale*, which was undersigned in 1933 by Funi, Carrà and Campigli.[14] Its opening statement was: "Fascism is a style of life: the very life of Italians." This programmatic text impressed the idea of the social function of art that needed to translate and interpret the Fascist ethic of its own time, subordinating the individuality of a single originator to the needs of the collective. If for Sironi mural art needed, with reference to the past, to become the instrument of spiritual government, the ethical importance and the historical dignity attributed to the style distanced it from a propagandistic system generally

Adalberto Libera, Antonio Valente, *Sanctuary to the Martyrs. Exhibition of the Fascist Revolution*, from *Guida della Mostra della Rivoluzione Fascista*, 1932

[10] See E. Prampolini, "Futurismo: Arte della Rivoluzione fascista", in *Futurismo*, I, no. 10, 13 November 1932, p. 4 and I, no. 12, 27 November 1932, p. 3; E. Prampolini, "Artisti futuristi e futuristizzati alla Mostra della Rivoluzione Fascista", in *Dinamo Futurista*, I, no. 1, February 1933.
[11] M. Sarfatti, "Architettura, arte e simbolo alla mostra del fascismo", in *Architettura*, XII, no. 1, January 1933, p. 10.
[12] See *Mostra Augustea della Romanità: Catalogo*, Rome, 1937.
[13] Regarding the *Arengario* by Maraini, and in general regarding the works in the Wolfson Collection inspired by the idea of *romanità*, see M. Fochessati, "Il senso del passato", in S. Barisone, M. Fochessati, G. Franzone, *La visione del prisma: La Collezione Wolfson*, Palazzo Pilotta, Parma, 1999, pp. 21-46.
[14] M. Sironi, "Pittura murale", in *Il Popolo d'Italia*, 1 January 1932; republished in *L'Arca*, III, no. 1, April 1932 and in *Domus*, V, no. 1, May 1932. M. Sironi, A. Funi, C. Carrà, M. Campigli, "Manifesto della Pittura murale", in *La Colonna*, December 1933.

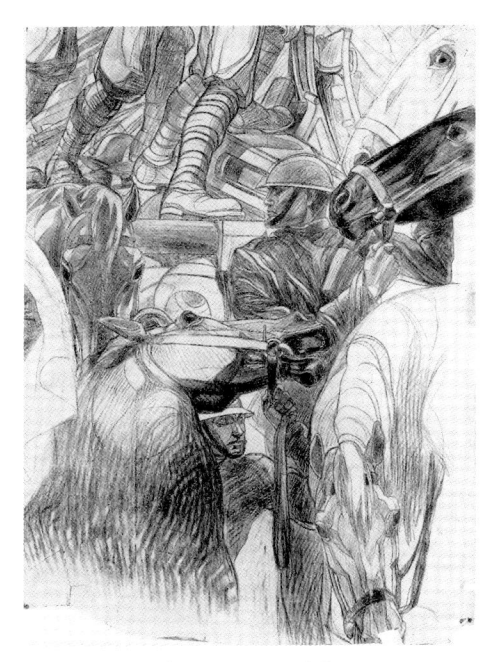

Duilio Cambellotti, *Triptyc of the Victory (detail). Study for decorations in the Palazzo del Governo in Ragusa*, 1933

imposed on contents exalting national values. In the sphere of the management of public patronage a link between the borrowings from Italy's artistic tradition and the celebration of mythical models from the past was already establishing itself in the preceding years, as can be seen from the preparatory studies for the friezes in the Sala Consiliare del Palazzo della Provincia in Arezzo (cat. nos. 35-36), executed between 1922 and 1924 by Adolfo De Carolis.[15] The epic celebration of themes such as soil and toil are depicted in this pictorial cycle, displaying clear similarities with the themes of Fascism's rural propaganda, which in the common need to return to tradition, tuned itself into the vernacular culture that had had an impact on the entire oeuvre of Duilio Cambellotti. Inspired by the humanitarian socialism of Tolstoy from the turn of the century onwards, the Roman artist, flanked by a group of intellectuals and painters composed of Giacomo Balla, Giulio Bargellini, Aristide Sartorio, Giovanni Cena and Sibilla Aleramo, was preoccupied with the social problems of the Roman countryside as is evident from his organizational efforts for the *Mostra dell'Agro Romano*, inaugurated at the Ponte Flaminio for the occasion of the *Esposizione Internazionale* of Rome in 1911. The primary iconographic motifs of this work, which aimed at elevating the standard of life for the masses, can be found in his important decorative scheme for the engineer Cesare Brunetti's Palazzo dell'Acquedotto Pugliese in Bari (cat. no. 39), which he was involved in from 1931 to 1934.[16] A clearer adhesion to propagandistic themes of celebration can be found in his murals for the Palazzo del Governo in Ragusa (cat. no. 41), built to the design of the architect Ugo Tarchi between 1929 and 1931. In light of the imposition of the subject matter – a synthetic representation of the advent of Fascism from Vittorio Veneto's victorious episode to the March on Rome – the artist's autonomy of expression was limited solely to questions of execution and technique, Cambellotti insisting on the use of tempera where fresco had been requested.[17] Then again, the cases of artists bowing to the rhetoric of the regime are numerous in these years, as is demonstrated, for example, by Galileo Chini's designs for a planned Palazzo delle Corporazioni (cat. nos. 44-45).[18] Internationally acclaimed for his frescoes in the cupola of the vestibule of the Venice *Biennale* (1909) and for the Throne Room in Bangkok (1911-13), Chini had already realized two large panels for the decoration of the Italian Pavilion of Armando Brasini at the Paris exhibition of 1925, depicting work in the fields, and in 1940 he worked on a number of cartoons on an analogous theme for a House of the Peasant in Bologna.[19] There is no definite information regarding the execution of the paintings. A mood of celebration also inspired the mural decorations of the Aeronautical Ministry in Rome, inaugurated in 1931 and conceived by Italo Balbo who was head of the ministry from 1929 to 1933, and who entrusted the project of the monumental building to the engineer Roberto Marino. The works, of which here are exhibited a few designs from the archives of the ebanist Luigi Carugati, who collaborated with the Milanese architect Meraviglia Mantegazza on the realization of the interior design, illustrate in a graphic and analytically descriptive style the legendary aeronautical feats of Balbo (cat. no. 40). This visually enhanced the rhetorical emphasis of the slogans on the walls.[20] The aeronautical enterprise, prestigiously undertaken by the future Governor of Libya who, in 1933, led a squadron of twenty-five seaplanes in the famous transatlantic flight which was so triumphantly received in Chicago, was one of the most recurrent themes of propaganda under Mussolini. The successes accomplished by Italian aviation and celebrated by the *Esposizione Aeronautica Italiana*, inaugurated in Milan at the Palazzo dell'Arte in 1934, contributed, in fact, to the diffusion of the image of a technologically avant-garde Italy and to reinforce the Fascist cult of hardiness, danger and sporting victory as a military metaphor.

It is not odd, therefore, that in the official catalogue for the *Chicago World's Fair*

---

[15] The preparatory cartoons are also in the Wolfson Collection; see S. Barisione, M. Fochessati, G. Franzone, *La visione del prisma*, cit., pp. 37, 140 and 188.
[16] See M.P. Maino, G. Pediconi, *Il Palazzo dell'Acquedotto Pugliese*, Rome, 2001.
[17] See M. Quesada, "Cambellotti e il ciclo di Ragusa", in L. Sciascia, *Invenzione di una prefettura: Le tempere di Duilio Cambellotti nel Palazzo del Governo di Ragusa*, Milan, 1987, pp. 155-89.
[18] See F. Benzi, "Galileo Chini affreschista e decoratore", in *Ad vivendum: Galileo Chini. La stagione dell'Incanto. Affreschi e grandi decorazioni 1904-1942*, Terme Tamerici, Montecatini Terme, 2002, p. 90.
[19] *Ibid*.
[20] The Carugati archive, part of the Wolfson Collection, has a series of photographs of the interiors of the ministry building. See also G. Morolli, "Il Ministero dell'Aeronautica," in F. Borsi, G. Morolli, *I Palazzi della Difesa*, Rome, 1985, pp. 197-248.

of 1933, *A Century of Progress*, Italian participation – whose fulcrum was represented by the project of Adalberto Libera and Mario De Renzi's pavilion, in which the dynamic lines of a transatlantic ship were symbolically combined with those of an aeroplane and a locomotive – received the following commentary: "The voice of modern Italy, vibrant with the heroic deeds of Fascism, speaks more resoundingly, more intelligently and more forcefully to the World's Fair visitor than that of any foreign nation participating in *A Century of Progress*… Progress is the keynote of modern Italy and the long and romantic history of the Italian peninsula pales before Italy's plans for the future. The very design of the building is symbolic of the epoch-making flight of General Italo Balbo, who led an armada of seaplanes from Italy to the Fair."[21]

That sense of inferiority on the international stage that seemed to have characterized Italy's recent history before the advent of Fascism, as witnessed by Filiberto Scarpelli's 1924 poster *Italy Abroad* (cat. no. 9), seemed to have now been defeated and overcome. Even so, this winning image imposed by a propaganda that, via the organization at home of a series of uninterrupted thematic shows and the participation in many exhibitions abroad, amplified the echo of the large public works undertaken by the regime, was not to withstand for long the impact of political and military dynamics which inflamed the international political scene throughout the 1930s.

The sanctions taken against Italy by the Society of Nations following the attack on Ethiopia (1935-36) renewed Italy's isolation, determining the beginning of economic and cultural autarchy. It is precisely on these grounds that Fascist propaganda, imposing a transformation in the consumer habits of Italians, spent all its energy in tightening the nation in the face of this new emergency. This campaign for economic self-sufficiency, which had been started by the so-called "Battle for Grain", culminated in the *Mostra Autarchica del Minerale Italiano* held in Rome in 1939 at the Circus Maximus. Unravelling itself over a sequence of twenty-six pavilions dedicated to the industrial activities connected with the extraction and working of minerals the exhibition, which was organized by Cipriano Efisio Oppo, saw the participation of some of the most important Italian artists of the time, such as the Futurist Enrico Prampolini, who with his spectacular installations proposed a scenographic and emotionally engaging elaboration of the theme of the exhibition.[22] By this time the framework for all exhibitions was the imperial dream within which the Fascist regime had enclosed itself – as demonstrated by the structure of Michele Busiri Vici's Italian Pavilion at the *New York World's Fair* of 1939, of which the Wolfson Collection owns the wooden model. However, the regime was unable to fulfil its most ambitious project of self-representation. The anticipated *Esposizione Universale* of 1942, the last large concrete enterprise of Mussolini's propaganda machine, did not take place because of sudden military action.

The big event was sadly substituted in the same year by a modest recreation at the National Gallery of Modern Art in Rome of the *Mostra della Rivoluzione Fascista*, in the hope of reviving the celebratory mood of years past.

Esposizione di Chicago. Italian Pavilion, 1933

[21] *Foreign Participation: Colorful Italy*, in *Official Guide: Book of the Fair 1933*, Chicago, 1933, p. 92.
[22] The Wolfson Collection conserves the two designs by Enrico Prampolini: *Bozzetto per salone centrale del Padiglione dell'Autarchia nella Mostra del Minerale*, 1939, tempera, pencil and collage on paper (GD1993.47.1) and *Padiglione Autarchia Dettagli Strutturali I*, pencil on tracing paper (GX1993.513).

Santagata and Salietti: Two Examples of Mural Painting from the Wolfson Collection between the "Fascistization" of Italy and the Collapse of the Regime

Franco Ragazzi

Marcello Piacentini, *Casa Madre dei Mutilati, Hall from the Apse*, Rome, 1928, from U. Nebbia, *La Casa Madre dei Mutilati in Roma*, 1928

In the years when Italy was "under Mussolini" every aspect of society, culture and art was in some way "Fascistized." After taking over the government of the country through a bloody civil war and a military coup d'etat, Fascism had put together a "technology of power" based on the suppression of all forms of democracy and the "organization of consensus" through the press, radio, cinema, the management of work and free time, welfare, education and the arts. It was a system which, as far as the arts were concerned, succeeded in being repressive and persuasive at the same time, with the result that in Italy every artistic group or movement, from "Futurists to still-lifers" (to use the categories of the aeropainters) came to consider itself more Fascist than the others in an attempt to put itself forward as the single most suitable artistic expression of the regime.[1]

There were, however, exceptions: Lionello Venturi did not wish to adhere to Fascism and left Italy; critics like Edoardo Persico and Attilio Podestà strove to look towards the experience of other countries. At least until the civil war in Spain there were arguments over poetics, not politics. The great "isolated" artists like Carrà, Morandi, Casorati, de Chirico, Savinio, the *Sei di Torino*, the Lombard *Chiaristi*, the *Astrattisti*, the Roman School and the young artists of *Corrente*, all gave voice to an art which, before reaching a critical attitude towards Fascism, reacted to the classical realism of the Novecento.[2]

Naturally, this sort of race to be considered the true artistic expression and the real, as it were, "official" artistic movement of Fascism, was something which the regime shrewdly went along with, supporting everyone without favouring anyone in particular. Apart from the frenzy of Farinacci and the *Premio Cremona* – through which the basest elements of Fascism tried to assert a Nazi aesthetic, aiming to import into Italy the campaign against "degenerate art" – the Fascist organization of consensus was largely based on a paternalistic attitude, in accordance with which artists operated in an atmosphere of apparent freedom, without an obvious aesthetic "direction" being set. Instead, there was a much more effective mechanism for persuasion and conditioning which came about not by means of a State art, but through a practice of government based on considerable financial commitment and an efficient organizational apparatus, in essence made up of a Fascist trade union which it was obligatory to join in order to take part in exhibitions, prize competitions, obtain professional appointments and assignments, take part in the acquisition of works of art through museums or public bodies and participate in the numerous public competitions for monumental sculpture and mural paintings.

---

[1] On issues of a general character see F. Tempesti, *Arte dell'Italia fascista*, Milan, 1976; various authors, *Gli Anni Trenta: Arte e cultura in Italia*, Palazzo Reale, Milan, 1982. For the political-cultural debate see P. Barocchi, *Storia moderna dell'arte italiana: Manifesti polemiche documenti*, vol. III, book I, *Dal Novecento ai dibattiti sulla figura e sul monumentale 1925-1945*, Turin, 1990.
[2] See D. Morosini, *L'arte degli anni difficili (1928-1944)*, Rome, 1985.

The impressive quantity of public works carried out in Italy in order to get over the economic crisis at the end of the 1920s, create work and modernize the country, and the great debate about the relationship between the new architecture and the visual arts, and in particular mural painting, were characteristic of Italian art in the 1930s and brought about, even though based on different premises and ideological aspirations, a significant coincidence of expressive and linguistic methods with the contemporary experience of Mexican and Soviet artists, and artists of the American New Deal.
After the mural experiments of Gerardo Dottori (Ostia Seaplane Base, 1928-29), Achille Funi (*IV Triennale* of Monza, 1930), Mario Sironi (Corporations Ministry, Rome, 1931) and the *Mostra della Rivoluzione Fascista* (Rome, 1932), generally considered to be the standard bearer of Italian mural painting, the debate throughout 1932 and 1933 had been punctuated by the conceptual system of Mario Sironi with a series of articles published in 1932 and the subsequent *Manifesto della Pittura murale*,[3] a confirmation and theoretical definition of the extraordinary mural event that was the *V Triennale* of Milan (1933). At the same time numerous artists of diverse sensibility found themselves, like Sironi, suffering from the "now restricted and inadequate form" of painting and pursuing the idea of an art which was renewed and total, restored in a modern way from old techniques, present in the everyday life of people in the city and integrated with the new architecture, capable of developing a didactic function suitable for ideological programmes and Fascist propaganda and of "capturing the attention in the public of this time of magnificent myths and gigantic upheavals."[4]
The ideas of Sironi and the experience of the *V Triennale* were followed with considerable attention by the regime: in the space of a few years it led to an exceptional distribution of professional commissions for the decoration of public works in every part of Italy and to the law, still in force today, of the "two per cent."[5]
The Mitchell Wolfson Jr. Collection/Fondazione Cristoforo Colombo in Genoa, through the diverse material – studies, sketches, cartoons, contemporary photographs, publications – related to Italian mural painting in the Fascist era, presents two examples which illustrate in a substantial way the beginning and end of the entire experience. These are the sketches by Antonio Giuseppe Santagata for the Casa Madre dei Mutilati di Guerra in Rome and the sketches worked on by Alberto Salietti for the Palazzo dei Congressi at the *Esposizione Universale di Roma* (also referred to as E42).

Antonio Giuseppe Santagata
The Casa Madre dei Mutilati, designed by Marcello Piacentini for the bank of the Tiber, between the Castel Sant'Angelo and the "Palazzaccio" of Justice, was built after 1925 to house the national seat of the Association for Disabled and Invalid War Veterans (ANMIG), an authentic "lay order" (in 1922 it had 500,000 registered members, 250 sections and 2500 subsections) created and headed by Carlo Delcroix, a symbolic figure of the political and cultural climate of the time.[6] The Casa Madre was the centre of an extremely powerful organization for welfare and propaganda recognized as "one of the most active forces in Italian life,"[7] but above all it was to be a kind of temple or a memorial chapel, a "monument to survivor heroes," modelled on the cult of death, of the fallen in battle, of victory, as well as the personality of Delcroix who lived there and dedicated to it his own energy and financial resources and those gathered from the members of the Association. The Casa Madre was constructed in two blocks, the first inaugurated in 1928 for the tenth anniversary of the end of World War One, the second in 1936 on the occasion of the proclamation of the empire. All the artists called upon to bring about the complex decorative programme were dis-

Antonio G. Santagata, *Carlo Delcroix*, c. 1928

[3] The *Manifesto della Pittura murale*, signed by Mario Sironi, Carlo Carrà, Massimo Campigli and Achille Funi, was published in the magazine *La Colonna*, edited by Alberto Savinio, in December 1933.
[4] M. Sironi, "Pittura murale", in *Il Popolo d'Italia*, 1 January 1932.
[5] The allocation of a percentage of the cost of the construction of public buildings for works of art, already announced in a circular by Mussolini in 1933, was to become the normal practice in the following years and became law in 1942.
[6] Carlo Delcroix (Florence 1886 - Rome 1977), after having oscillated between nationalism, syndicalism and interventionism, took part as a volunteer in the World War One when he was gravely wounded, losing his sight and hands. From 1924 to 1943 he was President of the Association for Disabled and Invalid War Veterans - Associazione Nazionale Mutilati e Invalidi di Guerra (ANMIG). He was elected to Parliament as a Deputy in 1924. His relationship with Fascism, initially uncertain, from 1925 became one of real "enthusiasm." In 1928 he published the biography of Mussolini *Un uomo e un popolo* and in the same year joined the Fascist party with all the members of the Association. In 1929 he entered the Chamber of Fascists and Corporations. At the end of the 1930s he took a critical attitude towards the regime and after 8 September 1943 was arrested for anti-Fascist activity. A politician, organizer, poet, historian, formidable orator and author of texts in which human sacrifice assumes mystical and sacred forms, he dedicated his life to the mystical representation of heroic death, the cult of victory and the Association for Disabled and Invalid War Veterans. See A. Vittoria, *Dizionario Biografico degli Italiani*, ad vocem "Delcroix Carlo", Rome, 1988, vol. 36, pp. 471-77.
[7] *Enciclopedia Italiana*, ad vocem "Delcroix Carlo", Rome, 1931, vol. XII, p. 518.

abled veterans, members of the Association, and as such, after 1928, also members of the Fascist party.[8]

Antonio Giuseppe Santagata[9] – who knew Delcroix very well and had collaborated for some time with the Association[10] as one of many artists working on the Casa Madre, despite an initially unfavourable reaction on the part of Piacentini – won the prestigious task of providing the frescoes for the most mystical and symbolic space, the Assembly Hall.

The strength of the ties which bound the Genoese painter to the President of the Association became apparent when, a few years later, a biography of the artist was written: "When the construction of the beautiful seat of the Association in Piazza Adriana was decided upon, a heated discussion arose within the executive council regarding the mural decoration of the great hall, which Santagata had offered to paint with frescoes. Certainly, painters can be capable and intelligent in a square metre of canvas, but painting tens and tens of metres, perhaps even hundreds of metres of whitewashed walls in a solemn atmosphere as austere as that of a cathedral, means taking on a task of exceptional responsibility… Opinions on the executive council were clearly in conflict, also because the architect had a damnable fear that fresco painting might harm the sober harmony of the place. Finally, the President was left to decide, and the President took the risk. Santagata got the commission for the decoration of the hall."[11]

The theme which Santagata worked on in the lunettes of the Assembly Hall was that of remembrance of heroic death in battle, of grief and of mutilation and the celebration of the soldiers' sacrifice, in the three episodes of *Departure*, *Assault* and *Return*, which gave life to as many great semicircular compositions, each of them divided into six compartments according to a "polyptych" model. The *Assault* was finished in time for the solemn inauguration of the Casa Madre on 4 November 1928, but the whole decorative programme for the Hall had already been worked out by Santagata, as Ugo Nebbia, who knew the artist, declared, noting that "the cartoons and the details of the studies were worked out in every detail."[12] Therefore, if one takes into account that Santagata finalized the sketches and cartoons in the years between 1926 and 1928, his frescoes for the Casa Madre could be considered the first great example of mural painting realized in Italy during Fascism, in the same years when Mussolini, through the special legislation of 1926 and the plebiscite of 1929, brought about the "Fascistization" of the country.

The composition for the *Assault* is divided up into two horizontal strips, with the lower one telling the story of a ferocious engagement through the episodes of the *Rush from the Trenches*, the *Fight* and *The Last of the Fallen*. In the upper part are the episodes of pity and grief: *Dressing Station*, *Transport for the Wounded* and *Pity on the Battlefield*, showing an infantryman bent over his dying comrade. The other lunettes and the apse, distinguished from the first by a greater rigidity and simplification of the figures, were finished by the end of 1932 and inaugurated on 15 January 1933 for the 8th Congress of Disabled War Veterans. In the cartoons and contemporary photographs of *Departure* it is possible to make out the portrait of Mussolini in the figure of the *Condottiero* which Santagata was to retouch in 1950 with the addition of a beard and moustaches. In the *Return*, amongst the figures following the soldier's coffin, Delcroix and Santagata himself appear. In the upper part is the large compartment of the *Canzone* in which a crowd of men and women, of the working class, veterans and harvesters are marching, in recollection of the *Fourth Estate* of Pellizza da Volpedo, towards a future symbolized by a little baby held high by the woman leading the procession.

There is a similar female figure who, instead of a baby, holds up to heaven a sword and an olive branch, standing out at the centre of the apse between a sentry and Carlo Delcroix who, in the tradition of Byzantine mosaics, holds up the

---

[8] On the Casa Madre, see R. Barbiellini Amidei, N. Cerino, S. Danesi Squarzina, G. Nifosì Sini, F. Matitti, *La Casa Madre dei Mutilati di Guerra*, Rome, 1993. Other than Santagata, the following worked on the Casa Madre: Ettore Colla, Arturo Dazzi, Edoardo Del Neri, Guido Galletti, Publio Morbiducci, Cipriano Efisio Oppo, Giovanni Prini, Romano Romanelli, Mario Sironi, Carlo Socrate and Adolfo Wildt. The Casa Madre still houses a considerable art collection.

[9] Antonio Giuseppe Santagata (Genoa 1888 - 1985) began his career in 1912, and in 1915 was a volunteer in the war where he was wounded. After a youthful symbolist phase he adopted the monumental language of the Novecento, making himself known in the 1930s as one of the artists most in harmony with the regime's requests for celebration. He took part in the Novecento exhibitions in Milan of 1926 and 1929; from 1926 he exhibited at the Venice *Biennale* where he was represented until 1942. After his success with the Casa Madre dei Mutilati of Rome he carried out numerous mural paintings. After the war he did the frescoes for the Eridania of Genoa (1951), the sanctuary Regina Apostolorum of Rome (1951-54), the Casa dei Mutilati of Milan (1953), the church of S. Paolo of Rome (1955), the Ospedale Galliera of Genoa (1958), the Guardia sanctuary above Genoa (1963-67), the church of Recco (1960-70). For his activity in the Fascist years see F. Ragazzi, "Cronache della pittura murale: Antonio Giuseppe Santagata, il 'Giotto dei soldati'", in V. Fagone, G. Ginex, T. Sparagni (eds), *Muri ai pittori: Pittura murale e decorazione in Italia 1930-1950*, Museo della Permanente, Milan, 1999.

[10] Santagata dedicated a portrait to Delcroix, exhibited at Genoa in 1922, as well as a marble bust housed at the Casa Madre of Rome, presented at the 1928 *Biennale*, of which a plaster cast is kept in The Wolfsonian-Florida International University of Miami Beach, exhibited in a bronze edition in Genoa in 1925 and intended for the Casa dei Mutilati d'Italia. Santagata illustrated the book *Sette santi senza candele* (Florence, 1925) for Delcroix. From 1923 the artist produced several medals and illustrations for the Veterans' Association.

[11] F. Petriccione, "L'arte di Anton Giuseppe Santagata", in *La Vittoria*, no. 8, June 1941.

[12] U. Nebbia, *La Casa Madre dei Mutilati in Roma*, Rome, 1928, p. 35.

Antonio G. Santagata, *The Sailor*, 1942

Antonio G. Santagata, *The Spanish Legionary*, 1936-38

Antonio G. Santagata, *Casa Madre dei Mutilati, Apse,* Rome, 1926-32

model of the Casa Madre.[13] In the *Offering of the Casa Madre to Victory*, the artist achieved a strongly unified composition, liberated from the confining structure of the lunettes, a composition of great evocative power in which the suffocating weight of hagiography and the celebration of the personality cult of Delcroix are partly dissolved in an unreal, almost abstract atmosphere in which the nightmare of heroic death is sublimated in the mysticism of the place which recalls that of a religious temple.

In the exhibition there are two preparatory sketches for the fresco in which *Victory* has the wings which it was to lose in the final version: the first still burdened with concessions to detail (the sentry box for the infantryman, the little church-sanctuary for the donor), the second – which was to be the definitive version – is more simplified, with the colossal figures almost separated, if one excludes a clod of earth on which they rest their powerful feet, from any reference to reality. Between the three giants liberated in space are represented the monuments symbolizing the cities "redeemed" by war (Trento, Trieste, Zara and Pola) and those Dalmatian cities still "unliberated" (Spalato, Traù, Sebenico and Ragusa).

Between 1936 and 1938 Santagata was to work again on the Casa Madre, painting frescoes for the walls of the portico of the Corte della Vittoria with battles fought by Italian soldiers from the trenches of Piave to the conquest of Abyssinia up to the Italian participation in the Spanish civil war, and painting Delcroix's private apartment with the view of the battlefields of *Piave and Col di Lana*.

At the conclusion of this "heroic cycle of frescoes" Santagata's success was remarkable and he earned a considerable fortune in the various War Veterans' Homes and in numerous public buildings in Italy.[14] After the unveiling of the first lunette the work was considered in a reading where artistic criticism had superimposed on it valuations of morality and recognition of the riskiness of the technical experiment: the press spoke of it as "a battle fully won by the combatant-artist."[15] Ugo Nebbia found "complete maturity of virtue" in the artist, by his skillful response to the "strict reasons" of architectural requirements with painting of high moral and aesthetic significance, capable of achieving something "so human, but at the same time such a lyrical commemoration of war."[16] These considerations of plastic, ethical and expressive force one finds persisting further in biographies dedicated to the artist and in the international press, where Santagata's painting was described as being "d'une prodigieuse puissance évocatrice."[17]

Alberto Salietti

With the work of Salietti for E42, one finds one of the last political acts of great power by the regime, consumed by the utopian idea of building a new city, a Fascist city, as a successor to that of Romulus, the Emperors and the Popes, a "fourth Rome" willed by Mussolini with the realization of the *Esposizione Universale di Roma* planned for 1942: a celebration and affirmation of the greatness of Italy on the twentieth anniversary of Fascism. An illusion destined to collapse tragically with Italy's entry into the war alongside Nazi Germany. In the great building sites of the exhibition there came about, or nearly came about, the ultimate experience of Italian mural painting in the years of Fascism with a great number of artists as protagonists.[18]

The story of Alberto Salietti[19] is a very significant chapter, with the recognition of a brilliant career punctuated by several successes also in the field of mural painting starting with the Milan *Triennali*, where Sironi had asked him to work from 1933 to 1936, the Palazzo di Giustizia in Milan, designed and directed by Piacentini (1938), the church of the Ospedale Maggiore of Milan (1939), in

---

[13] In the Wolfson Collection at Genoa, as well as two sketches for the *Offering of the Casa Madre to Victory* there is also the cartoon *Carlo Delcroix holds up the model of the Casa Madre*. In the same collection another two cartoons of Santagata are preserved: the stained glass window of the Casa del Mutilato of Genoa (1938) and *Cavalieri antichi*, a detail of the large fresco *Vita eroica di Antonio Locatelli* (1940) in the Casa Littoria at Bergamo.

[14] After the Casa Madre at Rome he executed frescoes for the Case dei Mutilati at Genoa (1938-39), Palermo (1939), Ravenna (1941) and Milan (1942). He decorated the chapel for the Institute for Blind War Veterans (Rome 1930-33) the Pavilion of Labour at the *Mostra della Rivoluzione Fascista* (Rome 1932), executed mural paintings for the local Fascist headquarters "Giordana" at Genoa (1933), the Rome Tram Company (1935), the November College of Ostia (1936), the Milan *Triennale* (1936), the Italian Pavilion at the Venice *Biennale* (1938), the Palazzo di Giustizia in Milan (1938), the Casa Littoria at Bergamo (1940) and the Ospedale of Gorizia (1942).

[15] "Le decorazioni di Santagata alla Casa Madre dei Mutilati", in *Oggi e Domani*, no. 41, January 1932.

[16] U. Nebbia, "Santagata", in *Emporium*, no. 445, January 1932.

[17] "Le culte des Héros dans l'Italie actuelle", in *La Chronique Hebdomadaire*, 2 December 1939.

[18] On the events at the Exhibition, see M. Calvesi, E. Guidoni, S. Lux (eds), *E42 Utopia e scenario del regime*, vol. II, *Urbanistica, architettura, arte e decorazione*, Archivio centrale dello Stato, Rome, 1987.

[19] Alberto Salietti (Ravenna 1892 - Chiavari 1961) grew up in a family of designers. In 1904 he followed his father to Milan where he attended the Accademia di Brera, and in 1915-18 he was a volunteer in the war. From being a painter of secessionist and "naïve" background, influenced by his activity as a childrens' illustrator, he adopted archaic forms, arising from his study of Giotto and Piero della Francesca, which brought him close to Carrà and the Novecento of which he became secretary in 1925. Later he turned towards impressionism and, with Arturo Tosi, would revitalize the naturalistic trend of the Novecento. He organized and took part in all the Novecento exhibitions in Italy and abroad, which brought him considerable fame. From 1920 to 1952 he took part in the Venice *Biennale* where he won the major prize for painting in 1942. He took part in the Rome *Quadriennali*, the Milan *Triennali* and several overseas exhibitions. After the war he lived and worked in Liguria. On his work see G. Giubbini, F. Ragazzi (eds), *Alberto Salietti: Un artista di Novecento*, Museo di Villa Croce, Genoa, 1997.

which he worked on the stained glass windows with Sironi and Aldo Carpi, and other large religious paintings.[20]

In the intensive programme of construction and decoration for the exhibition, it was anticipated that through a national competition there would be a gigantic mosaic decoration of almost 3000 square metres along the four walls of the Hall in the Palace for Receptions and Meetings, designed by Adalberto Libera.

When the competition announced in December 1939 concluded without winners, Cipriano Efisio Oppo, Vice President of the Local Board of the Exhibition, as well as a highly influential figure in the Italian artistic culture of the time,[21] personally invited, over and above those selected for the competition itself (the group made up of Quaroni-Capizzano-Gentilini-Guerrini, Grazia Fioresi, Dino Predonsani, the group Fornasetti-Majocchi-Ponti and Tommaso Cascella) also Achille Funi, Fausto Pirandello, Massimo Campigli, Aldo Salvadori, Giorgio de Chirico, Felice Casorati and Alberto Salietti. After refusals and withdrawals those who took part were Pirandello, Cascella, the group of Quaroni-Capizzano-Gentilini-Guerrini, Predonsani, Fioresi and Salietti.[22]

The themes which the artists had to work with had already been set in the national competition: "On four walls the following themes should be represented respectively: 1. *The Beginnings of Rome*; 2. *The Empire*; 3. *Renaissance and Universality of the Church*; 4. *Mussolini's Rome*. These themes may be illustrated by a symbolic composition or through the representation of a salient episode. However the artists should bear in mind that the Hall is conceived as the Temple, the Memorial Chapel of the idea of Rome, the fulcrum of our civilization." The Hall, with the four moments of history as protagonists of the decorative journey, therefore became not just the most representative space of the Palace but, through the explicit symbolic programme of the themes indicated, also the most significant, the real centre of ideology and propaganda of the entire exhibition, a monumental manifesto through which would come about the unveiling of Mussolini's ambitions for his "fourth Rome," the heir and successor to Imperial Rome, capable of declaring itself before the world with the force of Fascism and the Catholic faith. In the whole history of Italian mural painting, probably no other painting was invested with a similar role and such political, ideological and propagandistic content.

With the meticulousness which distinguished the artist, Salietti set to work filling up page after page of notes, starting up a sort of catalogue of historical subjects, figures, personalities, costumes, environments and quotations from works of art supporting the subjects which he sketched across hundreds of pages and pieces of paper. The sketches were turned into studies and from these into larger studies which were then sent to the competition.[23]

The artist worked at his task for months, asking for a postponement which Oppo would not grant him, and finally sent in his sketches, which were rejected by the commission who declared the victory of the Quaroni-Capizzano-Gentilini-Guerrini group. The precipitation of events in the war prevented the realization of the colossal work.

In fact, the judgement of the commission ratified the conclusion of the long debate about architectural decoration which had developed throughout the 1930s and during which the relationship between artist and architect had frequently assumed an antagonistic dimension. In this case, with the demands of propaganda, the architect won and the prize went to the project which had "taken most account of the needs of the architecture." It was noted how Adalberto Libera found these artists "tuned into the subordination of art and representation to the use of the architectural space." The report which declared the victory of the group underlined this aspect of "decorative work, which should be

[20] See F. Ragazzi, "La pittura murale e le grandi opere di Alberto Salietti attraverso *i cartoni preparatori* del Museo d'Arte Contemporanea di Genova e i documenti dell'archivio Salietti", in G. Giubbini, F. Ragazzi (eds), *Alberto Salietti*, cit. In the Wolfson Collection at Genoa, Alberto Salietti is represented by contemporary photographs and documents, as well as sketches for E42. The following cartoons donated by Rosa Devoto Copello in January 2001 are also held there: *Maternità* (Concorso Premi San Remo, 1936), *La Giustizia* (fresco, Palazzo di Giustizia, Milan, 1938), *Natività* (stained glass window, Chiesa Ospedale Maggiore di Milan, 1939), *Annunciazione* (mosaic, Santuario di Maria Bambina of Milan, 1953), *San Gaetano* (altarpiece, Chiesa di S. Gaetano of Milan, 1956).

[21] Cipriano Efisio Oppo (Rome 1890 - 1962), caricaturist, art critic, painter and set designer. After the World War One, he made a name for himself through his qualities as an organizer and, during Fascism, was the major representative of Italian artistic culture with political powers. With the support of Bottai he formed the National Fascist Trade Union for Artists where he held the post of Secretary General from 1926 to 1932. As well as being elected Deputy to Parliament in 1929, where he supported significant reforms of the national artistic system, he was Secretary of the Supreme Council of Fine Arts, artistic director of the *Mostra della Rivoluzione Fascista* (Rome 1932) and of the Fascist propaganda shows organized at the Circo Massimo (Rome 1937-38), a member of several prize juries, national and international exhibitions, and the organizer of shows of Italian art overseas. From 1931 to 1943 he was the originator and Secretary General of the Rome *Quadriennale*. In 1936 he was in charge of the Vice Presidency of the Local Board of the Universal Exhibition of Rome with responsibility for architecture, art and exhibitions. In 1941 he joined the Italian Academy. A valued artist, he was represented at exhibitions for the Secession in Rome, the Rome *Biennali*, exhibitions of the Novecento Italiano, the Venice *Biennali* and Italian art shows abroad, never abusing his political position to obtain personal privileges. On Oppo, see F.R. Morelli (ed.), *Cipriano Efisio Oppo un legislatore per l'arte: Scritti di critica e di politica dell'arte 1915-1943*, Rome, 2000, in particular the chapter "La vita 1890-1962", pp. 255-399.

[22] *Lettera di C.E. Oppo a A. Salietti*, Rome, 1 August XVIII (1940), Salietti Archive, Genoa. In the Archive the entire correspondence between the artist and the president of the exhibition is preserved – notes, preliminary studies, the announcement of the competition and related documents.

[23] Three of the definitive studies for the competition (except *Mussolini's Rome*) have been turned into mosaics and are conserved in the Galleria d'Arte Sacra dei Contemporanei di Villa Clerici in Milan-Niguarda.

Alberto Salietti, *The Beginnings of Rome*, 1940-41

Alberto Salietti, *Renaissance and Universality of the Church*, 1940-41

subordinate to the architecture," and indeed welcomed the "lack of a strong personality," whereas Predonsani, Salietti and Pirandello lost "precisely because of their autonomous and artistic quality".[24] If Fausto Pirandello lost because he did not believe "in the euphoric vision of the antique," it is sufficient to note the difference between Giovanni Guerrini's *Mussolini's Rome* and that of Salietti to understand the reasons for the latter's losing out, as his painting is so distant from the rhetorical and arrogant emphasis of the winner's: in the first, the protagonist was the mythology of the regime and attention to representing Party officials, and in the second, notwithstanding the set subject, it was the representation of the people.

The Wolfson Collection has preserved all of Salietti's research, the preliminary sketches and the four preparatory drawings for the definitive studies entered in the competition. On a gold background, as requested in the announcement, the artist developed a compositional scheme conceived along elementary lines, subdividing the space between a base section designed for narrative, and an upper level, almost empty to rebalance the mass. The narration takes place through the flow of scenes and personalities along parallel horizontal strips which have a good representation of saints and figures from the Ravenna mosaics loved by Salietti from boyhood, as he himself had written: "I was seven years old and

[24] S. Lux, "Il Concorso per 'La decorazione in mosaico nel salone del Palazzo dei Ricevimenti e dei Congressi'", in M. Calvesi, E. Guidoni, S. Lux (eds), *E 42 Utopia e scenario del regime*, cit., p. 339.

walked to San Vitale where the parish priest instructed me in the catechism; the beautiful mosaics of that church so captured my attention that it seemed to be teaching me something and those vague suggestions have followed me since then all my life."[25] The parades of figures were broken up by and integrated in architectural settings which historically fitted the different compositions: the temple of Capitoline Jove for *The Beginnings of Rome*, the Arch of Constantine for *The Empire*, St. Peter for the *Renaissance and Universality of the Church* and the arches of the new E42 under construction with the Colosseum in the background for *Mussolini's Rome*.

Oppo, in communicating to Salietti the decisions of the committee of which he was President, had to admit that his work was "judged worthy of interest and praise," and promised "to use for other work the artistic qualities demonstrated" by the artist as soon as a suitable occasion for a commission presented itself. In fact this happened shortly afterwards with the offer for the production "of a fresco picture for the Palace of Ethnography, not a large work, with a remuneration of thirty thousand lire."[26] A few days later the exhibition offices sent to Salietti the formal proposal for work on a wall of the Hall of the Museum of Popular Arts and Traditions, shared with four other artists (Domenico Colao, Mario Varagnolo, Emanuele Cavalli and Mario Gambetta) for which themes and sketches had already been approved. Salietti was offered the central and largest part of the composition with a subject which should "represent a scene characterized by its traditional and regional content." For Oppo the proposal to the painter of *Harvest* and of *Return to the Roots*, of *Ciociare* and *Women of Sardinia* must have seemed congenial although he had not set against this the difficult personality of the artist which made him refuse prestigious commissions and good remuneration to safeguard his own individuality and independence.

"I came to Rome on Monday believing it would be possible to decide with you on this work to be done for the E. U. (*Universal Exhibition*). Instead I find that it has all been decided, because I have received a parcel with the subject, the outlines for the walls and photos of the other sketches. I have been crucified!! There is nothing to find fault with, neither with the type of subject nor with the dimensions (I have no aspirations to fill up the huge walls) nor with the fee. But to feel myself *a priori* bound to other work already done, that everything is on the same wall, this is something which displeases me greatly. I feel myself already bound hand and foot and won't do anything worthwhile. Now I can't think of anything in my own way without the work of others spinning in my head. I'd be deceiving myself if I thought I could do anything just as I like it, I already saw it on a beautiful isolated wall and instead: disappointment!.."[27]

Notwithstanding the repeated invitations from Oppo, Salietti would remain firm in his decision. It is very likely that the disappointments suffered with E42 led the artist to renounce a little later the prestigious invitation to execute the frescoes for the University of Padua. Salietti, and with him many painters of his generation, considered the move towards mural painting attempted in the previous decade as having now definitely run its course.

[25] A. Salietti, "Gruppo di opere di Alberto Salietti", in *Seconda Quadriennale d'Arte Nazionale*. Palazzo delle Esposizioni, Rome, 1935, p. 104.
[26] *Lettere di C.E. Oppo a A. Salietti*, Rome, 4 February 1941, 15 March 1941, Salietti Archive, Genoa.
[27] *Risposta di A. Salietti a C.E. Oppo*, copy letter, Chiavari, 4 April 1941, Salietti Archive, Genoa.

The Decorative Arts in Italy from the Monza "Biennale" to the Milan "Triennale"

Silvia Barisione

Vittorio Zecchin, *Dining room, Three Venices Section*, I Monza *Biennale*, 1923, from *Emporium*, 1923

[1] P. Marconi, "Roma 1911: L'architettura romana tra italianismo carducciano e tentazione 'etnografica'", pp. 225-28, and A.M. Racheli, "Le sistemazioni urbanistiche di Roma per l'Esposizione Internazionale del 1911", pp. 248-54, in G. Piantoni, *Roma 1911*, Galleria Nazionale d'Arte Moderna, Rome, 1980.
[2] This theory was particularly promoted by the magazine *Architettura e Arti Decorative*, founded in Rome in 1921 and directed for the first six years by Gustavo Giovannoni and Marcello Piacentini.
[3] The *Biennali*, directed by Guido Marangoni (1923-1925-1927), had their centre in the Villa Reale at Monza, the work of the neo-classical architect Giuseppe Piermarini. See A. Pansera, *Storia e cronaca della Triennale*, Milan, 1978.
[4] C. Carrà, *L'arte decorativa contemporanea alla Prima Biennale Internazionale di Monza*, Milan, 1923, p. 18.
[5] R. Calzini, "Il programma delle Mostre", in "Il Congresso per la I Biennale Internaz. d'Arte Decorativa a Monza", in *Arte Pura e Decorativa*, vol. 1, no. 6, June 1922, p. 10.

The first attempt to renovate the Italian decorative arts with a programme that explicitly outlawed copying of the antique was the *Prima Esposizione Internazionale d'Arte Decorativa Moderna*, which was held at Turin's Parco del Valentino in 1902, and which confirmed the popularity of Art Nouveau within Italy in the fields of architecture and the decorative arts. Its pavilions – designed by the Friulian architect Raimondo D'Aronco – represented one of the most significant expressions in Italy of that *stile floreale* of Secessionist derivation which, by 1906, in that other great international exhibition, the *Esposizione del Sempione* of Milan, would be weighed down in the eclectic monumentality of Sebastiano Locati. By 1911 the *Esposizione del Cinquantenario* in Rome was to be a celebration of late Roman mannerism with the pavilions of Cesare Bazzani and Marcello Piacentini. On that occasion, organized to celebrate the fiftieth anniversary of Italian unification, the organizing committee requested that the individual designers in the section dedicated to the regional pavilions return to local traditions through references to historical styles. In the formal articulation of these buildings and their interior decoration, the continuity of an autonomous artistic tradition was evident, notwithstanding the recent constitution of a centralized State.[1]
In the following years this regionalistic inclination came to signify, on the one hand, a celebration and rediscovery of a vernacular architectural heritage[2] and, on the other, an attempt to awaken the sleepy Italian decorative arts, from the point of view of the popular arts, with the institution of the *Prima Biennale Internazionale delle Arti Decorative* at Monza in 1923.[3] According to the painter Carlo Carrà, its task was to "bring together the diffused impulses towards recovery developing in every Italian region, to incite our artistic industries to cherish our best workers and to discipline the movement for the redemption of our minor arts."[4]
Looking back to the example of the great Turin exhibition of 1902 which, despite many efforts, remained an isolated case, the exhibition at Monza was presented as a biennial review of the Italian decorative arts, the aim of which was to improve their quality by means of direct confrontation with products from around the world, which offered a worrying degree of competition on the domestic market. In the programme, Raffaele Calzini emphasized the importance of practicality and the elimination of academic virtuosity on the part of craftsmen. According to the critic, decorative art differed from pure art as "it should reach all the classes with its aesthetic function. Countries which are at the forefront of the renewal of the decorative arts also follow this rule."[5] It was not the promotion of luxury objects

that was needed, but simply of those in good taste. The "ancient and rustic" were excluded, although their importance was acknowledged as sources of inspiration for the renewal of the arts. Indeed, the motifs of rustic art "assimilated, transformed or employed by an alert artist"[6] were given particular prominence in the exhibition at Monza, from the regional sections – amongst which the Sardinian section stood out, coordinated by the architect Giulio U. Arata – to the foreign ones, in particular those of Russia, Czechoslovakia, Romania and Poland. In many ways, therefore, folkloristic elements acquired an important role in the context of innovation within the Italian applied arts. It was not, however, without its critics: Roberto Papini condemned the "rustic tendency, if this is to be solely understood as the rearrangement of simplistic and naïve motifs, upon which one aims to impose a semblance of aristocratic refinement."[7] In this respect he mentioned the furniture of the Venetian artist Vittorio Zecchin (cat. no. 21), created for the dining room of the Three Venices section, which "grafts an exquisite embroidery of incised, gilded lines onto shapes and planes of a primordial simplicity. One feels that this combination clashes, even though the acute sensitivity of this artist from Murano has wisely toned it down. The precious embroidery is not sufficient on its own to ennoble the rustic bulkiness of crude, simple shapes. A peasant dressed in gold will always be a peasant."[8] Papini thus sarcastically dismissed the affected contrast between the byzantine refinement of the gilded arabesques and the squared profiles of these pieces of furniture, painted black. In the field of practical and economical furniture made for a lower middle class market, the Tuscan critic pointed instead to the furniture in the Roman section designed by Vittorio Grassi (cat. no. 20), of which he wrote: "To the simplicity and elegance of the forms derived from English examples, he has added the preciousness of colouration and decoration with a few simple motifs, at times perhaps excessively repeated."[9] In the construction of his furniture, which slotted together and thus did away with the need for nails, Vittorio Grassi was evidently looking back to the example of the English Arts and Crafts movement; his predilection for painted wood related to studies on the use of colour and its impact on the human emotions.[10] Within the group of Roman artists, active in different fields of the applied arts, Vittorio Grassi, Duilio Cambellotti and Umberto Bottazzi had already dealt with themes related to the crafts, furniture and architecture from the time when they had worked for the magazine *La Casa*, founded in 1908 and dedicated to the "aesthetics, decoration and government of the modern home," with a particular emphasis on the issues surrounding popular architecture. Duilio Cambellotti was also a promoter of literacy amongst the inhabitants of the Roman countryside and spent a great deal of time teaching in rural schools.[11] At Monza his bulky, square pieces of furniture, inspired by the products of that region, captured the attention of the critics. *The Curious Ones* (cat. no. 18), a wall-mounted desk of walnut, exhibited in the study room of the Roman section, highlighted its rigorously compact refined shape by decorative detailing in the form of small bronze figures, symmetrically placed on the door to hide the handles and the lock. In his work, "often marked by genius," Agnoldomenico Pica recognized "a singular and independent 'rustic Romanism'"[12] whilst, according to Papini, his furniture proved "how starting from elementary structures or from an interpretation of natural forms one can attain unexpected and interesting results."[13] Two years later, at the *Seconda Biennale* of 1925, Papini was to define him as "one of the very few artists who has reached his own individual style which can be readily identified amongst thousands."[14] On that occasion, in the *Sala degli abitatori della campagna romana* (Room of the Inhabitants of the Roman Countryside), Cambellotti exhibited his small casket *Night* (cat. no. 19): four jambs in the shape of caryatids with the typical peasant hat emphasize the squared structure of the piece and frame a group

[6] *Ibid.*
[7] R. Papini, *Le arti a Monza nel MCMXXIII*, Bergamo, 1923, p. 38.
[8] *Ibid.*
[9] *Ibid.*, p. 40.
[10] See V. Grassi, "Camera da letto per signorina", in *La Casa*, II, vol. I, no. 10, 16 May 1909, pp. 184-85.
[11] At the *Esposizione Internazionale* of Rome in 1911 he had designed for the *Mostra dell'Agro Romano* the great central hut in which he exhibited, as well as the pieces of furniture made by peasants, his plaster models, pottery and temperas, alongside paintings by Giacomo Balla. See N. Cardano, *La mostra dell'Agro romano*, in G. Piantoni, *Roma 1911*, cit., pp. 176-98.
[12] A. Pica, *Storia della Triennale di Milano 1918-1957*, Milan, 1957, p. 14.
[13] R. Papini, cit., p. 43.
[14] R. Papini, "Le arti a Monza nel 1925: I. Dagli architetti ai pastori", in *Emporium*, vol. LXII, no. 369, September 1925, p. 152.

Melchiorre Melis, *Sardinian Smile*, 1929
(cat. no. 15)

Lino Berzoini, *Cherish Bread, the Sweet Smell of the Table*, 1935-38
(cat. no. 17)

Enrico Del Debbio, *A Provincial Party Secretary's Office in a Palazzo Littorio, Roman Section*, III Monza *Biennale* 1927, from *L'Arte Fascista*, 1927

Giuseppe Pagano, Gino Levi Montalcini, *Boardroom of a Company*, IV Monza *Triennale* 1930, from *Architettura e Arti Decorative*, 1930

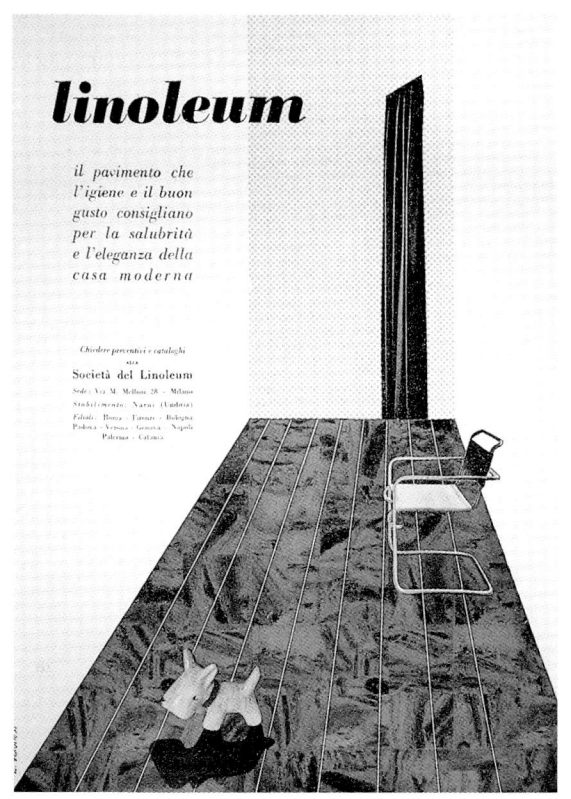

Italeum, advertisement from *Stile*, 1942

Luigi Veronesi, *Linoleum*, advertisement from *Edilizia Moderna*, 1938

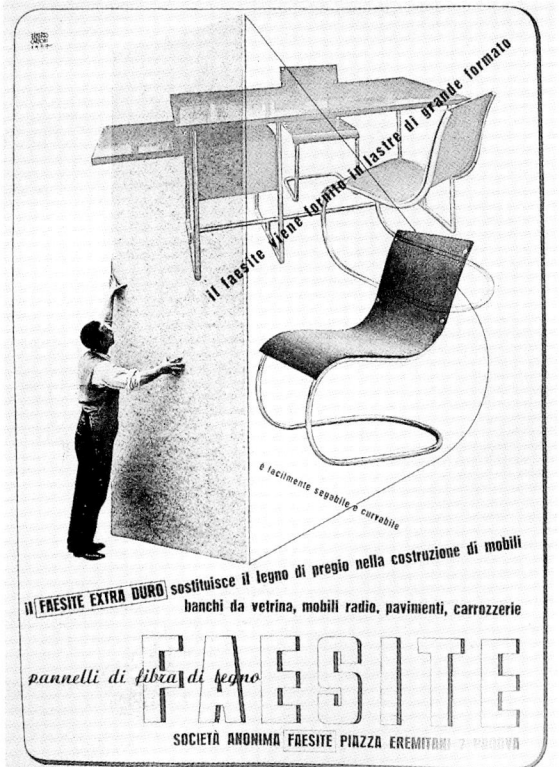

Erberto Carboni, *Faesite*, advertisement from *Edilizia Moderna*, 1938

Erberto Carboni, *Faesite*, advertisement from *Domus*, 1938

of sheep in ebony and ivory at its centre. Arguably his masterpiece, it represents the rustic world of Cambellotti suspended in a timeless dimension with barbaric, almost primordial overtones.

Amongst the pupils of Cambellotti in the Roman section was the artist Melchiorre Melis, who hailed from Cagliari. Looking back to popular Sardinian art, Melis managed to combine in his furniture and ceramics the folklore of his island and the geometrical characteristics of the international déco style. An example of this is the young girl in his *Sardinian Smile* (cat. no. 15), represented on a dish or ceramic tile, which featured at Monza in 1927.[15] The synthetic graphic design of the composition, played out in brilliant colours, reaches a further stylization in the frame, with its interlocking ears of wheat. The magazine *La Casa Bella* wrote about his ceramics in 1928, concluding that "the result could not be more encouraging. Even though the subject matter is rustic, the means of expression is refined."[16]

Towards the end of the 1920s the theme of rustic art was still popular in Italy. And yet in Paris by 1925 rural and folkloristic production had been strictly excluded from the *Exposition Internationale des Arts Décoratifs et Industriels Modernes*, the same year that a "place of honour" was reserved for it at the *Seconda Biennale* at Monza.[17]

However, by 1927, with the presence of the young architects of *Gruppo 7* and the installations of *Domus Nova* (Giò Ponti and Emilio Lancia) and *Labirinto* (Giò Ponti, Emilio Lancia, Tomaso Buzzi, Michele Marelli, Paolo Venini and Pietro Chiesa), the two principal architectural tendencies in Italy were represented – the Novecento and Rationalism – which eschewed regionalism. At the same time, the first signs of a Fascist art appeared, of which the most striking example was provided by the furnishings for a provincial party secretary's office in a Palazzo Littorio, conceived for the Roman section by the architect Enrico Del Debbio, who in the same year received the commission to design the complex of the Foro Mussolini in Rome. With regards to the project, the magazine *L'Arte Fascista* wrote: "This room has sparked the most acute interest by virtue of the national and contemporary significance that its overall shape contains, with its austere and imperious *romanità*."[18] It contained imposing, luxurious pieces of furniture in walnut, with ivory detailing, and a marble pedestal with polychrome inlay, crowned by a gilded bronze head of the *Duce*, the work of Attilio Selva. On the walls, three bronze bas-reliefs by the same artist celebrated the "greatest resources of the Italian people: *Genius, Work, Fecundity.*"[19] The leitmotiv of the *fascio littorio*, obsessively repeated in the furniture's carvings, in the fabrics and lamps, would, in the years to come, enter the iconographic repertoire of the regime and feature in the most varied artistic objects – ranging from those of everyday use, such as lamps (cat. no. 98) and clocks (cat. no. 97) to commemorative objects, such as the plates by Galileo Chini (cat. nos. 28-29) or the vase in Murano glass made in 1929 to celebrate the Lateran Pacts, which led to a *rapprochement* between Church and State (cat. no. 27). The Fascist government immediately showed itself keen to develop the applied arts, conscious of their importance in a country "short on primary resources but rich in the inexhaustible genius of a tenacious and fecund people,"[20] and it supported the National Committee for Craftsman and Small Industries (ENAPI) from 1927. This organization was to promote and direct the production of small companies according to the market's demands and establish a collaboration between the designer and the manufacturer. In 1930 the government extended its control over the activity which took place in the schools and art institutes through the magazine *Rassegna della Istruzione Artistica* which, directed by the Ministry for National Education, was to document and guide the work undertaken by their pupils.

---

[15] G. Franzone, "Per un'analisi del "ruralesimo" nella Collezione Wolfson: Da Cambellotti alla 'mistica rurale' fascista", in S. Barisione, M. Fochessati, G. Franzone, *La visione del prisma: La Collezione Wolfson*, Palazzo Pilotta, Parma, 1999, p. 70.
[16] E. Agostinone, "Arte rustica nella casa moderna", in *La Casa Bella*, I, no. 3, March 1928, p. 18.
[17] So wrote Guido Marangoni in the exhibition's programme. See A. Pansera, *op. cit.*, p. 166.
[18] A. Nosari, "Un gabinetto per un palazzo del Littorio alla Biennale di Monza", in *L'Arte Fascista*, II, no. 11, November 1927, p. 427.
[19] *Ibid*.
[20] Artifex, "L'Ente Nazionale per le Piccole Industrie e le Arti Applicate in Italia", in *Rassegna della Istruzione Artistica*, I, nos. 2-3, April 1930, p. 82.

During his visit to the *IV Esposizione* of Monza in 1930, the *Duce* appeared gratified with the results achieved by the small industries and through the "union which he desired to see between architects, designers and manufacturing artisans." Therefore, "he decided that this current exhibition would become triennial, and would also be recognized by the State. Since the Villa del Piermarini seemed unsuited to architectural installations of a modern character, he considered transferring the exhibition to Milan."[21]

The regime always maintained an ambiguous attitude toward modern art and architecture, adopting a policy of *trasformismo*, which enabled it to appropriate the most diverse stylistic tendencies, thereby guaranteeing a certain freedom of artistic expression within Italy. Mussolini hoped for a new State art that would, however, look back to the traditions of imperial Rome. In architecture, his taste oscillated between the rationalism of the architects of the *Italian Movement for Rationalist Architecture* (MIAR) and the *Novecentismo* of Marcello Piacentini.[22] With regard to the applied arts, he was concerned above all with their growth in relation to the development of the country from the point of view of craftsmanship and industry. Consequently, this cultivated a production midway between tradition and innovation, both sides of which the regime exploited as and when necessary. Corrado Cagli borrowed stylistic elements from Futurism to depict the March on Rome (cat. no. 1); the return to ruralism, promoted in the regime's propaganda following the laws instigating the "Battle for Grain" of 1925, was evident in the dish by Lino Berzoini entitled *Cherish Bread, the Sweet Smell of the Table* (cat. no. 17); references to *romanità* were manifest in the tile by Corrado Mancioli which was manufactured by SPICA for the *Triennale d'Oltremare* (Overseas Triennial Exhibition) held in Naples in 1940 (cat. no. 111) and the theme of the Spanish Civil War was apparent in the delicate bowl made by Golia for the Lenci company (cat. no. 96). Works of pure propaganda appeared alongside these artistic objects – the icon of the *Duce* being explored in formal and graphic approaches that were sometimes ingenious, as in the case of Renato Bertelli's *Continuous Profile of Mussolini* (cat. no. 85) or Buriko's portrait of the dictator reproduced on the dish *His Excellency the Honourable Mussolini* (cat. no. 84).[23]

In the field of interior design this same attempt to appropriate new developments on the part of the regime was clearly expressed in an article which appeared in 1937 in *ABC Rivista d'arte*: "After the Great War, Futurism and the Novecento impressed in every field, and therefore also in furnishing, a way of reacting against the hybrid nature of late nineteenth century art, a way which – under the impulse of Fascism – tended to bring pieces of furniture back to sober lines and smooth surfaces, this paving the way for the birth of a new style which, in its fusion of the Roman spirit and modern technique, may be defined as Roman-imperial."[24]

Leaving aside the ideological connotations which the regime's propaganda attempted to associate with the different movements, Carlo A. Felice presented the two principal architectural styles of Rationalism and Classicism as aspiring to a common "serene clarity, to a calm equilibrium of forms, to a sincere *italianità* and modernity of expression" in his volume *Arte decorativa 1930 all'Esposizione di Monza*.[25] In clarifying a concept of *italianità* that was not far removed from the assertions of the regime, Felice shook off the accusations of xenomania which had been directed at the architects of MIAR, who were accused of having slavishly followed the example of the German avant-garde. The Rationalists answered these criticisms by asserting that whilst aware of developments on the other side of the Alps, their architecture also referenced the vernacular architecture of the Mediterranean coast, with its essential forms, smooth walls without decoration and flat roofs. On the other hand, references to the architecture of the classical

Luigi Vietti, *Living room, Pavilion of Ligurian Architects*, V Milan *Triennale* 1933

[21] F. Sapori, *L'arte e il Duce*, Milan, 1932, pp. 178-79.
[22] See C. De Seta, "Cultura e architettura in Italia tra le due guerre: continuità e discontinuità", in S. Danesi, L. Patetta, *Il razionalismo e l'architettura in Italia durante il fascismo*, Venice, 1976, pp. 7-12; and G. Massobrio, P. Portoghesi, *Album degli anni Trenta*, Bari, 1978, pp. 116-20.
[23] G. Di Genova, *"L'uomo della provvidenza": Iconografia del duce 1923-1945*, Palazzo Mediceo, Serravezza, 1997, pp. 15, 84 (ill.).
[24] T. Rovere, "Il mobilio artistico attraverso i tempi", in *ABC Rivista d'Arte*, VI, no. 3, March 1937, p. 17.
[25] C.A. Felice, *Arte decorativa 1930 all'Esposizione di Monza*, Milan, 1930, p. 16.

Emanuele Rambaldi, *Chiavari's chair*, V Milan *Triennale* 1933, from *Domus*, 1933

tradition were inescapable in the work of the Milanese Novecento group, whose adherents stripped down and simplified Lombard neo-classicism.
One of the first manifestations of Rationalist architecture in Italy was the building designed for the Gualino offices in Turin (1928), commissioned from the young architects Giuseppe Pagano and Gino Levi Montalcini by the industrial patron Riccardo Gualino. The furnishings, displayed at Monza in 1930, included 77 different styles. Manufactured by the FIP company of Turin (Fabbrica Italiana Pianoforti), they constituted one of the first attempts at serial production in Italy, albeit on a reduced scale. Their formal structure evinced a deep understanding of the work of designers such as Robert Mallet-Stevens, of the De Stijl group and, in particular, with regard to the deep armchair (cat. no. 46), of Joseph Hoffmann.[26] The episode of the Gualino offices remained exemplary for its conceptual unity, as the furnishings were conceived of as integral to the planning arrangement of the interiors. The novelty of the materials used was also significant. Buxus, derived from the Latin name for boxwood, was an elastic yet solid material with a marble-like surface similar to briar wood which was obtained by a process of "ossifying cellulose" and could take on a vast spectrum of colours.[27] It represented one of the principal alternatives to wood, even though its use was mainly limited to the region of Piedmont. Only at the end of the 1930s was buxus relaunched through a collaboration between the Futurist from Trento, Fortunato Depero, and the Turinese industrialist Valentino Bosso. Unlike other new materials, buxus had not been widely promoted by magazines of the day. First among these other new materials was linoleum, made from linseed oil, resins and cork powder treated chemically. This was promoted in a major publicity campaign which focused on its hygienic, hard-wearing qualities and its ease of installation. The magazine *Edilizia Moderna*, founded in 1929, constantly promoted the use of this material, publishing examples of its applications in buildings and interior decoration. Invented in 1863 by the Englishman Frederick Walton and produced in Italy from 1898, it became one of the autarchic materials *par excellence*. The autarchic policy, introduced by the regime in 1936 in response to the economic sanctions imposed the year before by the League of Nations following the Italian invasion of Ethiopia, pushed for an increase in the national production of primary resources and led to a propaganda campaign exhorting the public to purchase and use only products made in Italy. In this context linoleum – although already used internationally by architects of the modern movement, its British origins long-forgotten – became one of the autarchic materials, together with other alternatives to wood such as eraclit, eternit, populit, faesite and masonite.[28] *Adagio con i mobili razionali* (Easy does it with Rationalist Furniture) was the title of an article in the *Rassegna della Istruzione Artistica*, which as early as 1932 had expressed its concern with regard to the increased production of pieces of Rationalist furniture in a country rich in carvers, but short on primary resources: "We have plenty of fine wood workers, experts in shaping, engraving, marquetry work and so on, and we are still educating them in our schools; but what are we going to do with all these workers, if we completely reject their ability? Shall we allow hard-won technical conquests and traditions to die out, simply to have people polish and shape luxury woods? And do we believe that we can resist the foreign competition, when the only things required of a piece of furniture will be the value of the materials, of the exotic woods that we neither have nor produce?"[29]
Following the first Milanese *Triennale* of 1933 architecture had attained a dominant position alongside the industrial and decorative arts. In the first triennial exhibitions of the 1930s the Rationalist tendency proved to be victorious. The different habitational modules scattered around the Palazzo dell'Arte of Giovanni Muzio, which referred back to the *Weissenhofsiedlung* of Stockhard, constructed

[26] A. Bassi, L. Castagno, *Giuseppe Pagano*, Bari, 1994, p. 56.
[27] Pagano and Levi Montalcini got to know the new material at the Turin *Esposizione* of 1928. The company of Giacomo Bosso which owned different factories in Piedmont on that occasion designed an environment in the classical Roman style. See E. Garda, *Il Buxus: Storia di un materiale autarchico fra arte e tecnologia*, Venice, 2000, pp. 71-75.
[28] M.C. Tonelli Michail, *Il design in Italia 1925/43*, Bari, 1987, pp. 90-91.
[29] R. Paribeni, "Adagio con i mobili razionali", in *Rassegna della Istruzione Artistica*, III, no. 5, September 1932, p. 229.

for the *Werkbund-Ausstellung* of 1927, awakened the interest of the international critics. "Modern European architecture has not been without its influence on the young Italian artist. We can recognize the elasticity of Le Corbusier and the severe dignity of Mies van der Rohe playing an important role. But all such influences are turned to thoroughly national account. Italy is well on the way to developing her own architectonic culture,"[30] wrote *The Studio*; while for *Art et décoration* the *V Triennale* "révèle une unité qui séduit. Elle est l'expression d'une volonté unique… Un ordre de recherches: trouver un style national, tenant compte du climat, du cadre, et des matériaux locaux, mettant à profit les plus récents procédés de construction et reflétant l'esprit d'un régime."[31]

With regard to interiors, design was evolving with an eye to serial production. In the pavilion of Ligurian architects – one of the examples of habitational modules with a stainless steel frame – the armchair designed by Luigi Vietti (cat. no. 49) recalled the chairs in birch wood designed by Alvar Aalto, in the Finnish section of the exhibition, in the use of curved wood. However, the architect from Novara highlighted the different strata of its laminated construction.

In *Domus*'s review of the decorative arts present at the *V Triennale*, Giò Ponti published Ugo Carà's chromed metal objects[32] (cat. no. 58), in which the influence of Futurism was apparent – a movement to which the artist from Trieste had briefly adhered – as were references to the Vienna school, and particularly to the work of Karl Hagenhauer.

In the furnishing section of the same *Triennale*, Giò Ponti awarded first place to a chair in maple wood with a padded seat and back, constructed by the Chiappe firm of Chiavari to a design of Emanuele Rambaldi, painter, decorator and designer of textiles and carpets (cat. no. 63). "This model," stated Ponti, "signifies style and true rationality, a sense of proportion between character and destination, a happy injection of local technical traditions into the contemporary renewal of the arts."[33] The lightness of Chiavari's traditional chair – which dates back to the beginning of the nineteenth century, and which inspired Giò Ponti's famous *Superleggera*, designed for Cassina in 1955 – was updated by Rambaldi through the example of the tubular furniture of the Bauhaus.[34] Used by many Rationalist architects even after the war in interior design schemes, particularly BBPR,[35] it formed part of that recuperation of natural materials more suited to the Italian craft tradition, which the regime had never abandoned, as it was the result of the inventiveness and skill of the fatherland: a fact which could not be forgotten during the years of autarchy.[36]

In the section of the *V Triennale* devoted to ceramics Giò Ponti, after having analyzed the ceramic artists of Albisola and the smaller workshops, directed his attention to the Società Ceramica Italiana di Laveno, directed by Guido Andlovitz, "a great industry of ours of beautiful technical and artistic tradition."[37] If the function of the biennial exhibitions of Monza with regard to the large industries had been the divulgation of new forms, now that these had been diffused, the function of the *Triennali* and these industries, according to Giò Ponti, lay in their "indication of a *superior* taste and aesthetic."[38] Through the study and knowledge of foreign examples[39] directed by "artists chosen according to specific criteria," the triumph of Italian ceramics throughout the world would be achieved. Guido Andlovitz represented in Italy one of the most successful collaborations between designer and industry in the production of Italian ceramics in the period before the Second World War. If during the 1920s Andlovitz was looking to the ceramics of the Wiener Werkstätte with a vernacular, decorative taste, that was also sometimes recognizable in some of Ponti's subjects (cat. no. 24), in the 1930s he reached a preference for essential lines, as in the service exhibited at the *V Triennale* (cat. no. 55), the formal elegance of

Guido Andlovitz, *Ceramics*, from *Domus*, 1934

[30] "Modern design in Italy", in *The Studio*, vol. CVI, no. 486, September 1933, p. 143.
[31] L. Cheronet, "La Ve Exposition Triennale de Milan", in *Art et Décoration*, August 1933, p. 245.
[32] For the plant holder see "I metalli alla Triennale", in *Domus*, VI, no. 67, July 1933, p. 396. The bowl was published in the article, "Alcuni oggetti d'arte di Ugo Carà", in *Domus*, IV, no. 48, December 1931, p. 112.
[33] "L'arredamento alla Triennale", in *Domus*, VI, no. 65, May 1933, p. 232.
[34] K. Mang, *Storia del mobile moderno*, Bari, 1998 (original title: *Geschichte des modernen Möbels*, Stuttgart, 1978), pp. 28-32.
[35] For the chair and armchair of E. Rambaldi see, for example, G. Ponti, "Un appartamento degli architetti Banfi, Belgioioso, Peressutti, Rogers", in *Domus*, XI, no. 128, August 1938, pp. 2-6.
[36] I. Rossi di San Polo, *Artigianato*, in *Torino e l'Autarchia*, Parco del Valentino, Turin, 1939, pp. 169-71.
[37] "Industrie italiane d'arte ceramica alla Triennale", in *Domus*, VI, no. 67, July 1933, p. 384.
[38] *Ibid*.
[39] "The references to the most interesting foreign productions are essential to Italian ceramics so that they can keep up with the times," from "Ceramiche di Winnicott", in *Domus*, X, no. 116, August 1937, p. 36.

General View of the Exhibition Grounds,
V Milan *Triennale* 1933, from *The Studio*, 1933

[40] E. Biffi Gentili, *La Commedia Ceramica: Guido Andlovitz a Laveno Mombello*, in E. Biffi Gentili, M. De Grassi, *Guido Andlovitz: designer e direttore artistico per quarant'anni di ceramica industriale italiana, 1923-1961*, Palazzo Regionale dei Congressi, Grado, 1995, p. 21.

which was equalled only by the objects designed by Ponti for Richard-Ginori (another successful collaboration). The comparison with Keith Murrey – suggested by Enzo Biffi Gentili[40] – who designed pottery for Wedgwood from 1932, elevates the figure of Andlovitz to the international scene, especially in terms of his production of monochrome vases with rigidly geometric forms, those concentric cones of strong colours, not far removed from the circular and spherical vases with opaque, monochromatic surfaces typical of the New Zealand designer.

Francesco Sapori, *L'arte e il Duce*, 1932
(cat. no. 3)

Giuseppe Bottai, *Politica fascista delle arti*, 1940
(cat. no. 4)

Dino Alfieri, Luigi Freddi, *Guida della Mostra della Rivoluzione Fascista*, 1932
(cat. no. 5)

Dino Alfieri, Luigi Freddi, *Mostra della Rivoluzione Fascista*, 1933
(cat. no. 6)

The Demographic Colonization of Libya: Propaganda, Art and Architecture

Gianni Franzone

The Italian Empire, c. 1938
(cat. no. 109)

At the beginning of year XVII [1938] twenty thousand Italian colonists will land in Libya to undertake the great task of land reclamation. For six months intense work has been carried out in order that demographic colonization may be achieved. Comfortable, rationalist farmhouses have been constructed, punctuating the vast expanses with their whiteness; farms have been prepared and property boundaries delimited; life-giving water has been drawn from the bowels of the earth and roads laid across the steppe and over the Gebel. New villages are being constructed which bear the names of heroes, martyrs, precursors and statesmen of the new Fascist Italy.

This typewritten comment was carefully placed on the back of many photographs in the section dedicated to the last phase of the Italian colonization of Libya in the archive of the journal *L'Azione coloniale*.[1] In actual fact, these few lines – almost an elongated caption to accompany the images which were published in many contemporary magazines, and not only specialist or Italian ones – contain the essence of that great political, economic, social and propaganda initiative of the Fascist regime, which led to the permanent transferal of around 30,000 rural Italians to the agricultural areas along the Libyan coast between 1938 and 1939. These colonists were often described, with great rhetorical emphasis, as "rural infantries," an "army of intrepid rural Fascists" or simply the "twenty thousand," in reference to those who had formed part of the first migratory wave of autumn 1938. It was to be an ambitious and difficult project beset with many complications, yet was achieved within an incredibly short space of time. Although it was to reveal itself bankrupt from an economic – not to mention ideological – point of view, it was nevertheless effected and presented in such a manner as to inspire great admiration both within Italy and abroad.

The aim of this essay is not so much to summarize the various phases of this "intensive demographic colonization" of Libya, which is amply recorded in the journals and publications of the day and reconstructed in-depth in various specialist studies which have appeared over the course of the last few decades,[2] but rather to explore the photographic documentation contained in the archive of *L'Azione coloniale* and other material in the possession of Genoa's Wolfson Collection in order to investigate in more detail the artistic and urbanistic-architectural dimensions of the entire operation, which played no small part in the propaganda surrounding it. In fact, whilst it is true that the undertaking was to fail miserably in the space of a very few years, and proved to be an abysmal black hole that swallowed up an exorbitant amount of State funds, it should be recog-

[1] The magazine *L'Azione coloniale*, directed by Mario Pomilio, was published between 1931 and 1944, firstly in Rome and later in Venice. The *Organ of the Italians of Africa*, as its subtitle stated, was the weekly journal of the Fascist Colonial Institute which, in 1937, became the Fascist Institute of Italian Africa (IFAI), the most important body dedicated to colonial propaganda within Italy. The Wolfson Collection owns the incomplete archive of the journal, which is currently being catalogued. It contains over 11,000 items, including photographs, newspaper cuttings and other documentary material.
[2] For all aspects of the "intensive demographic colonization" of Libya – including the technical

nized that from the strictly *artistic* point of view it led to a number of achievements that are in no way negligible. The villages constructed in Tripolitania and Cyrenaica are amongst the highest achievements of the regime in the sphere of colonial architecture. These were coloured by very different ideological and political premises – and thus very different *artistic* premises – to those which underpinned the regime's achievements in the other recently acquired lands of the empire (Ethiopia, Eritrea and Somalia). Italo Balbo's Libya – that is, the four coastal provinces of Tripoli, Misurata, Bengasi and Derna, rather than the vast desert regions lying to the south, whose destiny was to be very different – came to be known as the "Fourth Shore"[3], a territory which also from both the administrative and legislative points of view became part of Italy,[4] an extension of the fatherland, as it were, which had become too restrictive for the population and for that civilizing mission which Fascism considered had been assigned to it by history (an idea which was a central ingredient of the regime's propaganda). In Libya – the "pacified" Libya of the later 1930s, one must stress, when indigenous resistance had been suppressed by extremely violent means such as mass executions, deportations, concentration camps, and so on – the regime enforced (or rather, strove to enforce) a policy which, despite its strong limitations and many contradictions, may be defined as one of "assimilation" rather than "differentiation"[5], leading to some significant achievements from the artistic point of view. The architect and indefatigable organizer of demographic colonization, its most capable director by virtue of his undisputed promotional and managerial skills, was Italo Balbo, who became Governor of Libya on 1 January 1934. At that time, Balbo was at the pinnacle of his career. A "Fascist of the first hour," a former leader of violent Fascist gangs in Ferrara and a *quadrumvir* of the March on Rome, he had been Minister of Aeronautics, had achieved legendary status and world-wide fame as an aviator through his transatlantic mass-formation flights and had been promoted to the rank of Air Marshal.[6] Having arrived in Tripoli, Balbo set to work with his habitual energy. The idea of the demographic colonization of the coastal zones of Libya had not been entirely his: Luigi Razza and Alessandro Lessona had already striven to incorporate Libyan colonization into the programmes for domestic land reclamation and aid for the unemployed.[7] The Council for the Colonization of Cyrenaica (ECC) was already very active. This body – under the Ministry of Colonies and the Commissariat for Migration and Domestic Colonization (CMCI) – had begun work on the construction of the first four rural villages in the plain of Cyrene in December 1932: Beda Littoria, Luigi di Savoia, Giovanni Berta and Primavera (later renamed Luigi Razza in honour of the Council's president, who had died in an aviation accident). This already represented an attempt – strongly supported by the State – to link demographic colonization to that of the capitalist variety, and which foresaw the permanent transfer to the colony of Italian farmers. It was Balbo who created the legislative, administrative and technical framework that allowed this scheme to be translated into reality. One of his first initiatives was to bring about the administrative unification of Tripolitania and Cyrenaica[8] and to connect them physically with the construction of Litoranea, later named Balbia, which finally united Tripoli and Bengasi and therefore the entire country from the Tunisian frontier to the Egyptian border.[9] Without these two achievements the migration of the "twenty thousand" would never have been realized.

It is worthwhile emphasizing the fact that Balbo's project of colonization, with its promotion of the image of the independent farmer with his small holding, coincided perfectly with the aims of the regime at that time: namely, the creation of a "new man", the "Fascist man", a rural Italian, anti-urban and anti-industrial, bound to the earth and therefore easily controlled by the Fascist Party, devoted

Umberto Di Lazzaro, *Decennial Transatlantic Crossing*, special issue of *Le vie dell'aria*, 1933

and economic dimensions – see I. Balbo, "La colonizzazione in Libia", in *L'Agricoltura Coloniale*, August 1939, p. 464 onward; C.G. Segrè, *L'Italia in Libia: Dall'età giolittiana a Gheddafi*, Milan, 1978 (original title: *Fourth Shore: The Italian Colonization of Libya*, Chicago and London, 1974), pp. 100-201; A. Del Boca, *Gli italiani in Libia: Dal fascismo a Gheddafi*, Rome and Bari, 1988, 1991, pp. 233-326; F. Cresti, *Oasi d'italianità: La Libia della colonizzazione agraria tra fascismo, guerra e indipendenza (1935-1956)*, Turin, 1996, pp. 3-100.
[3] Italy has three coastlines, washed by the Tyrrhenian, Ionian and Adriatic seas. With the colonization of Libya it thus acquired a "fourth" Mediterranean shore.
[4] With the Regio Decreto Legge no. 70 of 9 January 1939 the four coastal provinces of Libya became an integrated part of the fatherland. Consequently, certain "qualified" Libyans were granted *piccola cittadinanza*, a kind of "second-class citizenship."
[5] For the concepts of "assimilation" and "differentiation" see L. Goglia, "L'imperialismo coloniale fascista", in L. Goglia, F. Grassi, *Il colonialismo italiano da Adua all'Impero*, Rome and Bari, 1981, 1993, p. 211 onward.
[6] Biographical information on Italo Balbo can be found in G. Buccicante, *Vita di Italo Balbo*, Rome, 1941; G.B. Guerri, *Italo Balbo*, Milan, 1984; G. Rochat, *Balbo*, Turin, 1986; C.G. Segrè, *Italo Balbo: Una vita fascista*, Bologna, 1988, 2000 (original title: *Italo Balbo: A Fascist Life*, Los Angeles and London, 1987).
[7] See C.G. Segrè, *L'Italia in Libia*, cit., pp. 112-17.
[8] See Regio Decreto no. 2012 of 3 December 1934.
[9] Work on Litoranea was concluded in February 1937.

Village of Giovanni Berta in Cyrenaica, the church (arch. Umberto Di Segni), c. 1934
Photo by V. Dinami, Bengasi

Village of Giovanni Berta in Cyrenaica, view of the centre (arch. Umberto Di Segni), c. 1934
Photo by V. Dinami, Bengasi

Village of Primavera (later renamed Luigi Razza) in Cyrenaica, the church and the presbytery, 1933-34
Photo by V. Dinami, Bengasi

Village of Oliveti in Tripolitania, panoramic view, c. 1938

to the regime and indebted to it for everything – house, land and work.[10] The premises at the root of the project for the draining of the Pontine marshes, and the consequent construction of the "new" cities,[11] were the same as those at the basis of the demographic colonization of Libya and the development of the rural villages. From the strictly architectural and artistic point of view the analogies between the two episodes are also striking, allowing for necessary distinctions due to the differences in scale and geophysical environment. In fact, the Fascist "rustic mysticism" which was being cultivated – with its image of a timeless, primitive and pre-industrial world and its idealization of the peasant as hard-working, industrious and obedient, triumphing over the adversity of nature through his efforts and remaining perfectly contented, thanking God and the *Duce* – is already present in these premises, even though such an image was only to find its most complete representation in the works submitted to the second *Premio Cremona* in 1940.[12]

Balbo's project underwent a notable acceleration from 1935 and even more so after Mussolini's visit to Libya in March 1937. The ECC, by this point transformed into the Council for the Colonization of Libya (ECL), and the National Fascist Institute for Social Security (INFPS), which Balbo had decided should work alongside one another, constructed a number of other villages between 1936 and 1938: Maddalena, D'Annunzio, Baracca and Battisti in Cyrenaica; Crispi, Gioda, Breviglieri, Oliveti, Giordani and Bianchi in Tripolitania.

The colony was now ready to receive the first 1800 families of settlers from the fatherland. They departed on 29 October 1938 from the ports of Genoa and Naples in a fleet of ships commandeered for the purpose[13] under the highly attentive direction of Balbo and the gaze, at once admiring and astonished, of a crowd of journalists, many of whom were foreign. A carnival atmosphere surrounded the event, which also brought to mind the Biblical exodus. For Balbo, this operation signified another international success. It would appear that the extent of the publicity surrounding it irritated Mussolini as the second migration had a much lower profile. This time the colonists left Italy between 28 and 30 October 1939 from the ports of Venice, Naples and Palermo, destined for Filzi, Sauro, Oberdan and Mameli in Cyrenaica and Micca, Tazzoli, Marconi, Castelverde, Corradini and Garibaldi in Tripolitania.

The planning of the villages was almost entirely entrusted to architects who resided *in situ* and worked almost exclusively on colonial projects. They included Florestano Di Fausto, Umberto Di Segni and Giovanni Pellegrini:[14] architects who in terms of their training, taste and attitude toward colonial architecture were very different but who nevertheless adopted similar stylistic approaches for the villages upon which they worked. Pellegrini was in fact the author of the *Manifesto dell'Architettura Coloniale* in 1936[15] in which, referring to the criteria to which architects were told to adhere in designing the new cities, he declared: "All of the solutions which indigenous constructions show to be efficacious (houses with central courtyards, walls without windows, narrow streets) should be utilized, being resolutely blended with that which modern techniques teach us and modern aesthetics demand." And again, "it is not useless to specify that by re-entering into tradition one means to push it forward and that so-called 'folkloreisms' should be absolutely excluded, as should the imitation of styles mistakenly considered traditional."[16]

The architectural criteria for the first four villages of Cyrenaica (Beda Littoria, Luigi di Savoia, Luigi Razza and Giovanni Berta) realized by the ECC in the two years 1933-34, established the guidelines on the example of which later villages would be modelled. The urban scheme adopted was based on traditional rural town planning, and the public buildings around which the life of the communi-

[10] On the relationship between urbanism and ruralism, with particular reference to architectural concerns, see R. Mariani, *Fascismo e "città nuove"*, Milan, 1976, particularly chapter II; and R. Mariani, "Trasformazi'ni del territorio e città di nuova fondazione: 'Ruralesimo' e città", in *Gli Anni Trenta*, Palazzo Reale, Milan, 1982, pp. 285-99.
[11] The "new" cities of the reclaimed Agro Pontino were Littoria (modern day Latina), inaugurated December 18 1932; Sabaudia, inaugurated 15 April 1934; Pontinia, inaugurated 27 December 1935; Aprilia, inaugurated 29 October 1937 and Pomezia, inaugurated 29 October 1939.
[12] For the 1940 *Premio Cremona* see G. Franzone, "Per un'analisi del 'ruralesimo' nella Collezione Wolfson: Da Cambellotti alla 'mistica rurale' fascista", in S. Barisione, M. Fochessati, G. Franzone, *La visione del prisma: La Collezione Wolfson*, Palazzo Pilotta, Parma, 1999, pp. 81-84.
[13] For the migration of the "twenty thousand" and the following migration of October 1939 see the already cited volumes by C.G. Segrè, A. Del Boca and F. Cresti. Regarding the reaction of foreign journalists, see M. Moore, *Fourth Shore: Italy's Mass Colonization of Libya*, London, 1940. Moore followed the story as a correspondent for London's *Daily Telegraph*. See also G.L. Steer, *A Date in the Desert*, London, 1939.
[14] Di Fausto was responsible for the villages of Maddalena, Battisti, D'Annunzio, Mameli and Oberdan in Cyrenaica and Oliveti in Tripolitania. Di Segni designed Berta in Cyrenaica and Breviglieri, Bianchi, Gioda, Micca and Tazzoli in Tripolitania. Pellegrini designed the village of Baracca in Cyrenaica and Corradini and Marconi in Tripolitania. The latter worked with Di Segni on the village of Crispi in Tripolitania. See P. Carbonara, "Recenti aspetti della colonizzazione demografica della Libia", in *Architettura*, XVIII, April 1939, vol. IV, pp. 249-60; and D. Ortensi, *Edilizia rurale: Urbanistica di centri comunali e di borgate rurali*, Rome, 1941, pp. 545-56.
[15] The manifesto, discussed and approved by the Inter-provincial Fascist Union of Lombard Architects, was published in *Rassegna di Architettura* in October 1936. See *Rassegna di Architettura*, VIII, October 1936, pp. 349-50 and Assoc. Cultori di Architettura del S.I.F.A. della Lombardia, *Problemi di architettura coloniale*, Milan, n.d. [1936], pp. 13-16.
[16] *Ibid.*

The "Twenty Thousand" greeting the new land from the ships, 1938
Photo by Bruni, Rome

[17] G. Gresleri, "La 'Libia felix' e i contadini di Balbo", in G. Gresleri, P.G. Massaretti, S. Zagnoni, *Architettura italiana d'oltremare 1870-1940*, Galleria d'Arte Moderna, Bologna, 1993-94, p. 304.
[18] O.C., "I villaggi agricoli nel Gebel di Cirene", in *Rassegna di Architettura*, VII, March 1935, p. 85. The article is signed "O.C." but the initials "A.C." appear on the contents page. The author is most likely to have been Ottavio Cabiati, a collaborator on the journal at the time and active in Libya. With Alberto Alpago-Novello he devised the town-planning scheme for Tripoli in 1932-33.
[19] C.E. Rava, "Di un'architettura coloniale moderna", in *Domus*, IV, no. 42, June 1931, p. 32.
[20] O.C., "I villaggi", cit., p. 85.
[21] V. Quilici, "La colonizzazione libica: Koiné mediterranea o contaminazione dei linguaggi?", in *Metafisica costruita: Le Città di fondazione degli anni Trenta dall'Italia all'Oltremare*, Complesso di San Michele a Ripa, Rome, 2002, p. 198.

ty revolved (church, Fascist meeting hall, town hall, school, infirmary or surgery, market, shops, stores, hostelry and carabinieri barracks, not all of which were always present in every village) were grouped around a central piazza that functioned as a focal point for the surrounding farms, which were frequently somewhat distant and isolated. Individual buildings "are treated with the freedom typical of the Rationalist urban approach: the 'modern style' is conceived as a workable 'simplification of the antique,' for this reason useable outside every conventional scheme, even within official guidelines."[17] In the March 1935 issue of the journal *Rassegna di Architettura* the following evaluation appeared: "These are constructions which have no architectonic pretensions and their merit is precisely in this modest, decorous and modern simplicity of form which renders them appropriate to their function and consonant with their surroundings. In this land modernity meets with the spirit of the most ancient tradition."[18]

The ongoing pursuit and clarification of the objectives of colonization was paralleled by a progressive simplification of architectural form. Like the farmhouses the principal and official buildings – which served a primarily symbolic role – became white, luminous masses, true geometric solids (in particular cubes and parallelepipeds) with elementary but articulated volumes and pure and essential forms, classical in their concision and without the least trace of decoration. Only long, deep porticoes, broad arcades and windows of various dimensions puncture and articulate the surfaces. It is "Mediterranean architecture" in the truest sense of the term, the most immediate precedent of which is the popular architecture found along the Mediterranean coast and defined in the celebrated words of Carlo Enrico Rava: "white cubes and sunny terraces beneath the bluest of skies."[19]

One is able to note the progressive process of simplification by comparing the first four villages to have been built in Cyrenaica with those constructed for the "twenty thousand." The colonial housing tends to be low-rise, rigidly square, with a flat roof. However, there is still room for some decorative detailing on the perimeter walls, the entrance doors and windows are surrounded by slightly projecting cornices and the façades are sometimes clad in a stone surface. Public buildings present some rounded forms, some hint of stairs, some motifs taken from academic tradition. Iron railings edge the flat roofs or enliven the boundary walls, which present pleasant decorative motifs. The village of Luigi Razza was to be the least essential and architecturally the most complicated, whilst the last of the four villages to be constructed (Giovanni Berta) designed by Di Segni, was to be closer to those which were to follow it. The above-mentioned article goes on: "The soundness of the thesis followed is revealed in a negative fashion by the fact that Primavera [Luigi Razza] – the village richest in unnecessary motifs, such as the exedra behind the church, the roof terrace on the presbytery and the showy iron fences – appears the least successful. On the other hand, the most recent one of Gubba [G. Berta], with its snow-whiteness, and purity and essentiality of form, provides real pleasure to whoever pauses to look at it."[20]

On an ideological level the adoption of formal models inspired by Mediterranean architecture served to convey a belief that the Libyan people could be assimilated into the fatherland due to shared cultural roots. As Vieri Quilici noted: "With the disembarkation on the African shore one did not witness only a colonial conquest, but also a culturally complex phenomenon, a sort of 'return to the roots,' or better still, a rediscovery of the roots. Something special occurred, something like the rediscovery of an identity. It was not so much a case, then, of exporting a language as of finding a common one which would interest both shores, those of the colonist and the colonized. The Pontine cities like the Libyan villages. Tripoli like Littoria. E42 like the Overseas Fair. The journal *Civiltà* like the journal *Libia*."[21]

Village of Oliveti in Tripolitania, the central piazza and the market under construction, c. 1938

Village of Oberdan in Cyrenaica, model (arch. Florestano Di Fausto), 1938-39
Photo by G. Pucci, Tripoli

Almost all of the photographs from the archive of *L'Azione coloniale* show the villages either undergoing construction or eerily deserted, or else decked with flags and artificially crowded on the occasion of some official ceremony or other with propagandistic motives, such as one of the numerous visits of the Governor, the conferment of diplomas of merit, and so on. Only rarely do these images capture everyday life in the villages, with their inhabitants going about their normal business. They are empty and silent, as if suspended in a metaphysical atmosphere full of mystery. And in fact this was the image of Africa that the regime intended to cultivate during the 1930s – certainly not an exotic, sensual, picturesque Africa, throbbing with light, colour, sounds and noises, and thus emotionally potent, but rather a Romanized Africa, "a metaphysical, grandiose, immobile Africa; not a primitive Africa, but a classical, Latin one, immersed in a timeless light and marked by monumental architecture that speaks of a past more alive than the present."[22] In sum, an Africa already redeemed by the Romans and now ready to be redeemed once more by the civilizing mission of Fascist Italy. Many of the works executed by that "court" of painters which Balbo gathered around himself during his Tripoli period articulated this cult of *romanità*. These artists included figures such as Achille Funi (who was undoubtedly the most significant figure of this circle) and Mimì Buzzacchi, a highly skilled painter and xylographer who had accompanied her husband Nello Quilici to the colonies.[23] It was Balbo himself who officially conferred on Funi the task of supervising work on the numerous frescoes which were to be executed, predominantly in the village churches. Following this, between 1938 and 1940, Funi and Pio Gardenghi (director of the journal *Libia* and a close collaborator of Balbo's) called friends and sympathizers to work in Libya – above all, figures active in Ferrarese and Milanese circles, but also Carlo Socrate, Mino Maccari and the abstract artists Mauro Reggiani and Gino Ghiringhelli. In 1940, Mimì Quilici Buzzacchi executed a fresco depicting the martyrdom of the Saints Felicita and Perpetua for the small church at Corradini, the study for which belongs to the Wolfson Collection (cat. no. 101). The scene has a strong scenographic quality to it which may reflect the influence of the classical tragedies promoted by Balbo and performed in the recently restored Roman theatre of Sabratha. The various groups of figures are strongly demarcated: at the centre stand the two saints, ready to be sacrificed, whilst on either side stand two groups of Roman soldiers and other individuals wearing togas, who observe the scene like a sort of mute chorus, whilst a lion enters the foreground. From the sky appears an angel holding a palm leaf, the symbol of Christian martyrdom. Inevitably, ruins and columns with an archeological flavour and of clear classical inspiration appear round about, but mostly in the background. Certainly, one cannot say that this stage-like scene has not been constructed with study and notable artifice. Nevertheless, the expressions and gestures of the individuals are very naive, rendered in accordance with an excessively narrative taste and informed by an evident didactic intention. One tends to agree with Giuseppe Marchiori, who spoke of the work's "delicate innocence," and noted that "the altarpiece truly seems to be a votive picture, similar to those seen in *capitelli* or at the crossroads of country lanes, and which peasants decorate with wild flowers placed in rough glass vases or rusty tin cans."[24]

Some Futurists were also captivated by the Libyan enterprise. The Wolfson Collection owns Renato Di Bosso's painting *In Flight Above the Colonial Village "M. Bianchi"* (cat. no. 100) datable to 1938. Seen from an aerial perspective and at high speed the low, square buildings of the snow-white rural centre designed by Di Segni for the INFPS overlap and interpenetrate one another (the building in the foreground is the same as that which we find in the background). The depic-

---

[22] E. Pontiggia, "L'idea del classico: Il dibattito sulla classicità in Italia 1916-1932", in E. Pontiggia, M. Quesada, *L'idea del classico: Temi classici nell'arte italiana degli anni Venti*, Padiglione d'Arte Contemporanea, Milan, 1992, p. 22.

[23] For those artists active in Tripoli during the 1930s and the early 1940s, particularly those belonging to Ferrarese circles, see L. Scardino, "*L'officina* ferrarese in Libia: Funi e gli altri", in G. Gresleri, P.G. Massaretti, S. Zagnoni, *Architettura italiana d'oltremare*, cit., pp. 289-99.

[24] See G. Marchiori, "L'arte dell'affresco in Libia sotto il governo di Balbo: Le ultime chiese affrescate", in *Libia*, IV, nos. 5-6-7-8, May-August 1940, pp. 75-76.

tion of these buildings which is simultaneously dynamic and synthetic shows us that alternation of solids and voids, of clear, bright surfaces and deep, dark recesses, which is one of the salient characteristics of the Libyan villages, against the background of a landscape dominated by earthy tones of orange and brown, as if dried by the sun, which contrast with some touches of light green – almost a symbolic homage to the efforts that the colonists were making to transform the desert into cultivated land.

Mimì Quilici Buzzacchi must have only just finished her fresco in Corradini's tranquil chapel when Mussolini decided to take Italy to war alongside her German ally. The Libyan front immediately became caught up in the conflict. On 28 May 1940 Italian anti-aircraft fire brought down Balbo's aeroplane in the skies over Tobruk, this having been mistaken for an English bomber. In this manner one of the most controversial figures produced by Fascism prematurely met his end. The May-August 1940 issue of the journal *Libia* was entirely dedicated to Balbo, a duly reverent hagiography of that "Fascist hero" who seemed to be of more use to the regime dead than alive. Balbo himself would not have been able to find words more apt than those of his friend Pio Gardenghi to summarize his principal undertaking in the African territories: "One may remember, in conclusion, that the Libyan colonization had the character of the ancient Hellenistic migrations, of migrations which created, for example, the fabulous ancient Cyrene. The colonists till and valorize the soil, not desultorily or with a commercial or exploitatory spirit, but for their families and for their future, defending and consolidating the new fatherland which is a prolongation of the ancient glorious Italian fatherland. The *twenty villages* and agricultural centres already constructed vibrate with a healthy, simple, joyous and fertile life. Around these, *four thousand houses* for four thousand colonial families extend for as far as the eye can see, housing a total of *thirty-five thousand* farm workers. An impressive figure achieved through the migrations of the years XVII and XVIII."[25] Historical events have revealed the extent of the illusion and distortion, if not quite falseness contained within this testimony. The "Fourth Shore" of the "twenty thousand" did not outlive its demiurge for long: the dream of Balbo and the colonists lasted less than a total of four years. The Cyrenaica of the first rural villages in particular was to undergo two Italo-German offensives and three English counter-offensives in the space of three years. The colonists abandoned their villages and attempted to reach Tripoli, from where they hoped to sail for Italy. Almost as a cruel trick of destiny, the only Italian emigrants to have left their native land amidst joyous scenes and with the blessing of the State were to be those who returned home the soonest, utterly empty-handed.

The "Twenty Thousand" just landed at Tripoli raising posters, extolling the Duce, 1938

Italo Balbo delivering the house key to the head of a family, 1938

[25] P. Gardenghi, "Il testamento di Balbo", in *Libia*, IV, nos. 5-6-7-8, May-August 1940, p. 7.

Catalogue

Corrado Cagli, Dante Baldelli , *XXVIII October - Believe Obey Fight - In Silence and Strict Discipline - Combat*, 1931-32 (cat. no. 1)

Marcello Dudovich, *For Italy in the Name of the Dead!*, 1924
(cat. no. 8)

Leonetto Cappiello, *National Competition for the Victory of Grain*, 1926
(cat. no. 12)

Cesare Andreoni, *The Battle for Grain*, c. 1935
(cat. no. 13)

Dino Martens, *Vase*, c. 1932
(cat. no. 16)

Domenico Rambelli, *Agricultural Work*, 1926
(cat. no. 14)

Duilio Cambellotti,
The Curious Ones, 1923
(cat. no. 18)

Duilio Cambellotti, *Night*, 1925
(cat. no. 19)

Vittorio Grassi, *Seat*, 1923
(cat. no. 20)

Vittorio Zecchin, *Armchair*, 1923
(cat. no. 21)

Duilio Cambellotti, *Nightlight with owls*, 1924
(cat. no. 22)

Giulio Rufa, *Vase with octopus*, 1922
(cat. no. 23)

La Salamandra, Perugia, *Vase*, 1930
(cat. no. 25)

Gio Ponti, *Vintage*,
c. 1929
(cat. no. 24)

Ivos Pacetti, *Tea service*,
1929
(cat. no. 26)

Galileo Chini, *Iustitia et pax osculantae sunt*, 1929 (cat. nos. 28-29)

Salviati & Co., Venice (attributed to), *Reconciliation between the Church and the Italian State: 11-2-29-A.VII*, 1929 (cat. no. 27)

Aldo Buttini, *Young Boy with Scroll*, c. 1933
(cat. no. 31)

Eugenio Baroni, *The Sail*, c. 1933
(cat. no. 32)

Antonio Berti, *Portrait of Paola Ojetti*, 1935
(cat. no. 34)

Mario Palanti, *Study for "The Sarcophagus of the Martyrs"
in the Chapel of the Fallen, Palazzo del Littorio, Rome*, 1934
(cat. no. 33)

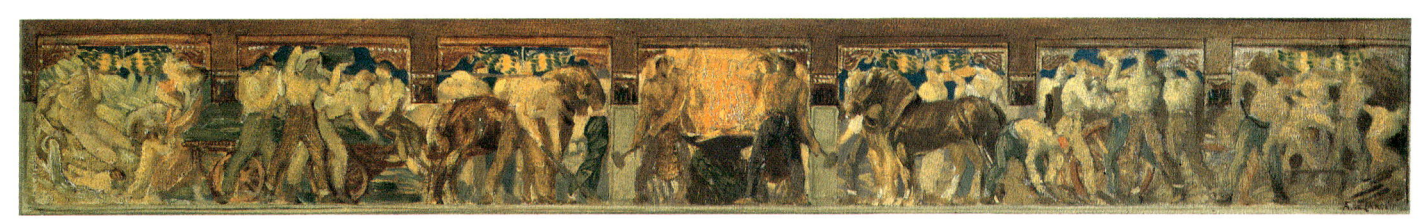

Adolfo De Carolis, *Working in the Mines. Study for the friezes in the Hall of the Provincial Council of Arezzo*, 1922 (cat. no. 35)

Working in the Fields. Study for the friezes in the Hall of the Provincial Council of Arezzo, 1922 (cat. no. 36)

Antonio Giuseppe Santagata, *The Offering of the Casa Madre to Victory. Study for the fresco in the apse of the Assembly Hall of the Casa Madre dei Mutilati di Guerra in Rome*, 1926-32 (cat. no. 37)

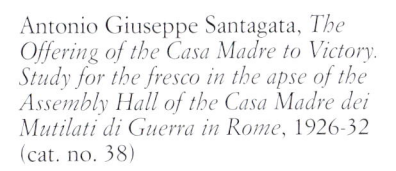

Antonio Giuseppe Santagata, *The Offering of the Casa Madre to Victory. Study for the fresco in the apse of the Assembly Hall of the Casa Madre dei Mutilati di Guerra in Rome*, 1926-32 (cat. no. 38)

Alberto Salietti, *The Empire. Study for the competition "Mosaic decoration in the Hall of the Palace of Receptions and Conferences", E42, Rome*, 1940-41
(cat. no. 42)

Alberto Salietti, *Mussolini's Rome. Study for the competition "Mosaic decoration in the Hall of the Palace of Receptions and Conferences", E42, Rome*, 1940-41
(cat. no. 43)

Duilio Cambellotti, *Washerwomen. Study for decorations in the Palazzo dell'Acquedotto Pugliese in Bari*, 1931
(cat. no. 39)

Duilio Cambellotti, *Triptych of the Victory. Study for decorations in the Palazzo del Governo in Ragusa*, 1933
(cat. no. 41)

71

Galileo Chini, *Construction Work*, c. 1935
(cat. no. 44)

Galileo Chini, *Steelworks*, c. 1935
(cat. no. 45)

Luigi Vietti, *Armchair from the Andrea Doria maritime station in Genoa*, 1933
(cat. no. 49)

Giuseppe Pagano, Gino Levi Montalcini, *Armchair for the Gualino Offices in Turin*, 1928
(cat. no. 46)

Marcello Piacentini, *Seats for the entrance hall of Fiammetta Sarfatti's house in Rome*, 1933
(cat. nos. 47-48)

Romeo Bevilacqua, *Game of Billiards*, 1932-34
(cat. no. 51)

Romeo Bevilacqua, *Motorcyclists*, 1932-34
(cat. no. 52)

Primo Sinopico, *Plate with skyscrapers and aeroplane*, c. 1930
(cat. no. 50)

Dante Baldelli, *Vase with archers*, 1933-34
(cat. no. 56)

Nicolaj Diulgheroff, *Vase*, c. 1932
(cat. no. 53)

Ivos Pacetti, *Vase*, c. 1933
(cat. no. 54)

77

Guido Andlovitz, *Coffee set*, 1933
(cat. no. 55)

Luigi Genazzi, Milan, *Centrepiece with plate*,
c. 1935
(cat. no. 59)

Ugo Carà, *Plant-holder*, 1933
(cat. no. 58)

Ugo Carà, *Bowl*, 1931
(cat. no. 57)

Giò Ponti, *Soup tureen*, c. 1936
(cat. no. 60)

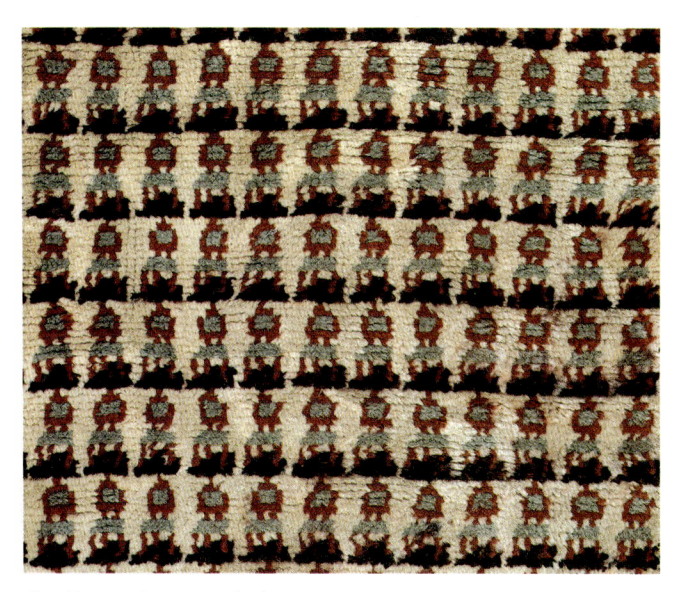

Giò Ponti, *Carpet with chairs*, 1935
(cat. no. 61)

Emanuele Rambaldi, *Carpet design*, n.d.
(cat. no. 63)

Alberto Bevilacqua, *Study for the "Wrestlers" carpet*, 1929
(cat. no. 62)

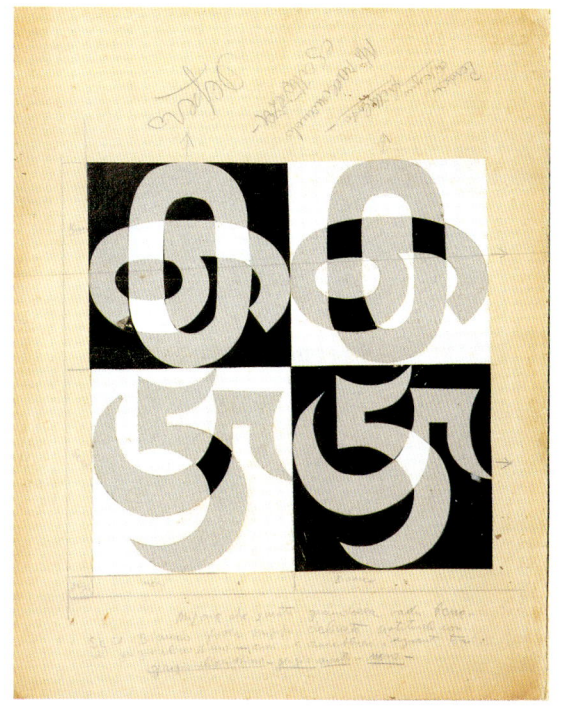

Fortunato Depero, *Carpet design*, 1927
(cat. no. 64)

Atla, *Barbisio Handmade Hat*, 1933
(cat. no. 67)

Giovanni Mingozzi, *Barbisio*, 1936
(cat. no. 71)

Atla, *Verelyte: "The Great Headscarf". Barbisio*, 1933
(cat. no. 68)

Sepo, *Noveltex! Evening*, 1936
(cat. no. 69)

Sepo, *Noveltex Sport*, 1936
(cat. no. 70)

Huge Reductions - Lama Italia, 1941
(cat. no. 72)

Erberto Carboni, *Boschi Luigi & Sons*, 1926
(cat. no. 65)

Alf Gaudenzi, *The Waiter*, 1933
(cat. no. 66)

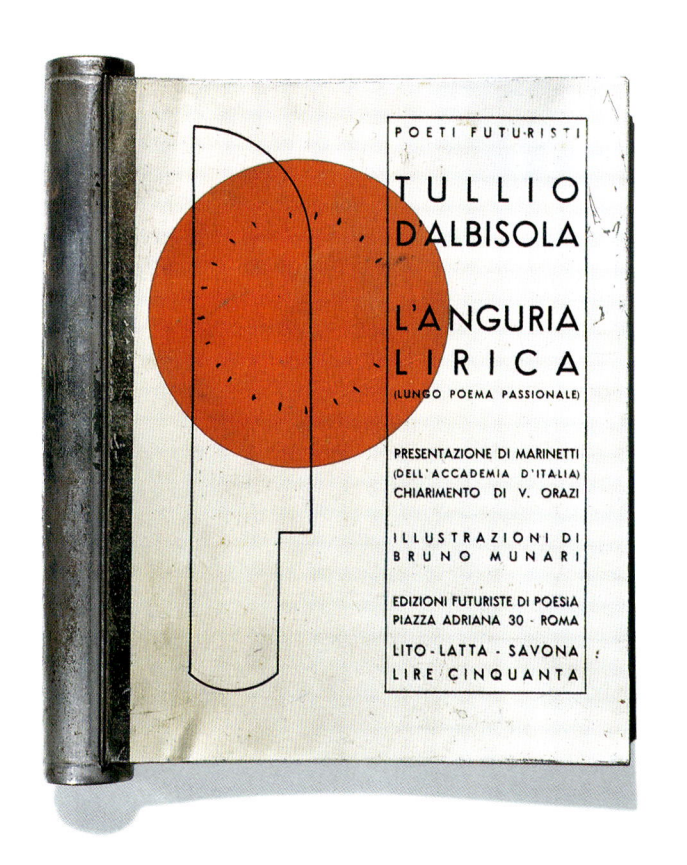

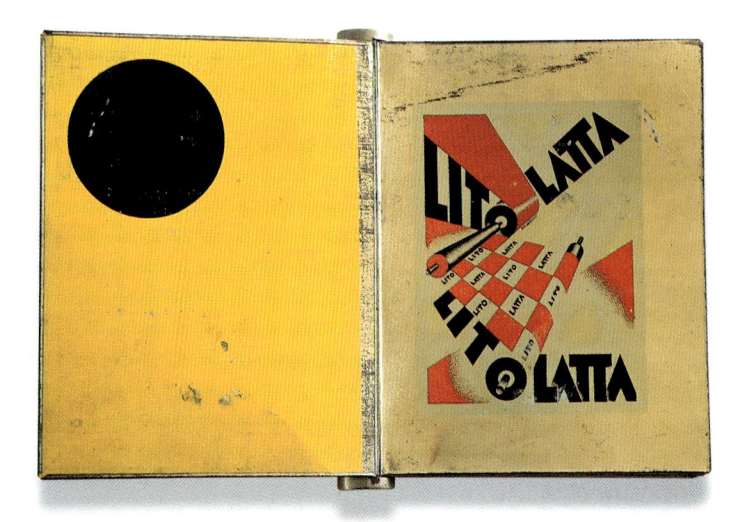

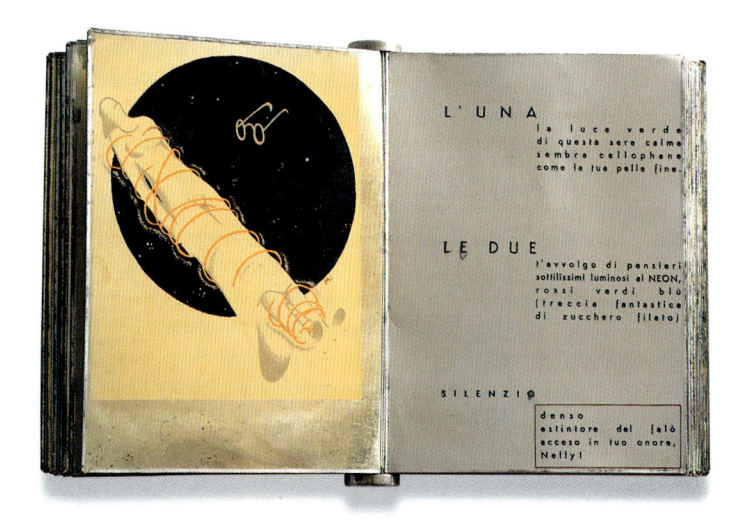

Tullio D'Albisola, Bruno Munari, *L'anguria lirica*, 1934
(cat. no. 73)

Ubaldo Cosimo Veneziani, *Portrait of a Mother and Child*, c. 1935
(cat. no. 74)

Verossì, *Balilla*, 1937
(cat. no. 75)

88

Gino Boccasile, *25 July*, 1943
(cat. no. 80)

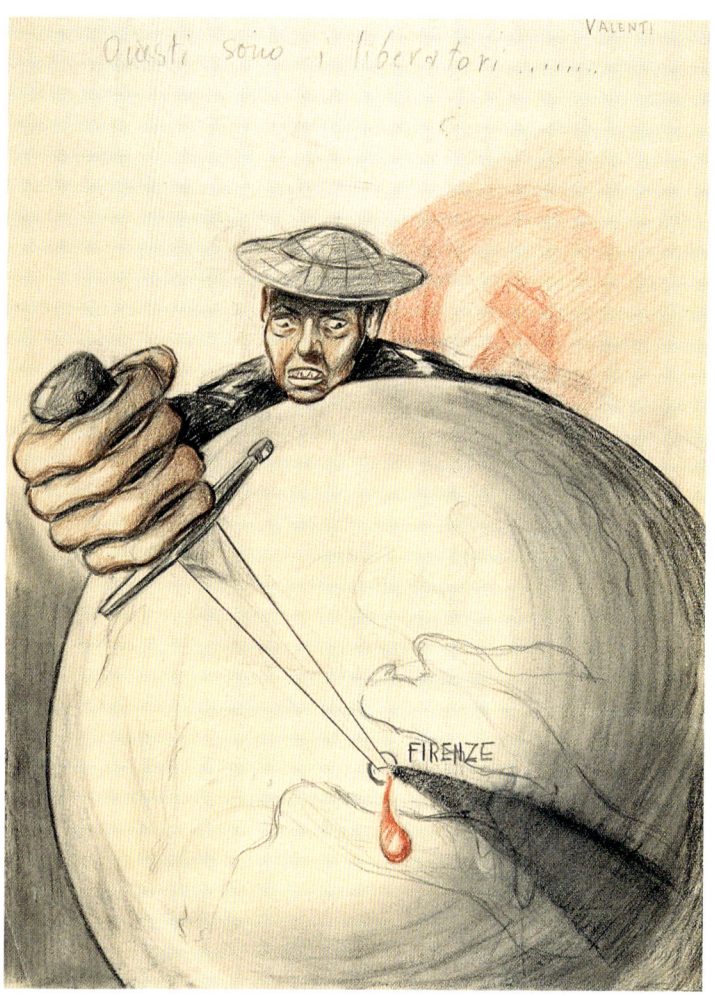

Valenti, *These are the Liberators*, c. 1943
(cat. no. 81)

Mario Sironi, *The Soldier and the Worker*, 1943
(cat. no. 79)

Renato Bertelli, *Continuous Profile of Mussolini*, 1933
(cat. no. 85)

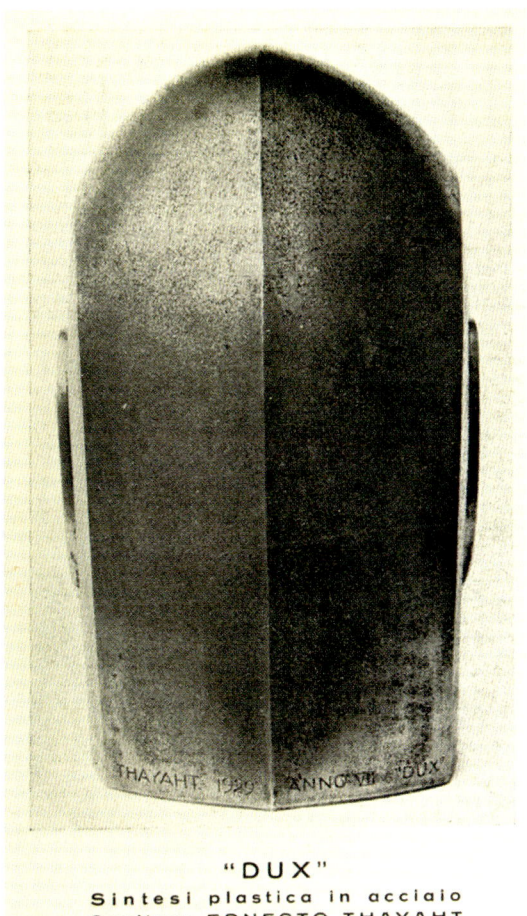

"DUX"
Sintesi plastica in acciaio
Scultore ERNESTO THAYAHT
Firenze   1929-VII

SMI, Florence, *Mussolini and Victor Emmanuel III*, 1939
(cat. no. 86)

G. Giannini, Florence, *Dux: Plastic synthesis in steel by Ernesto Thayaht*, 1929
(cat. no. 93)

Ernesto Thayaht, *Rome Year X. First Meeting of Professionals and Artists*, 1932
(cat. no. 95)

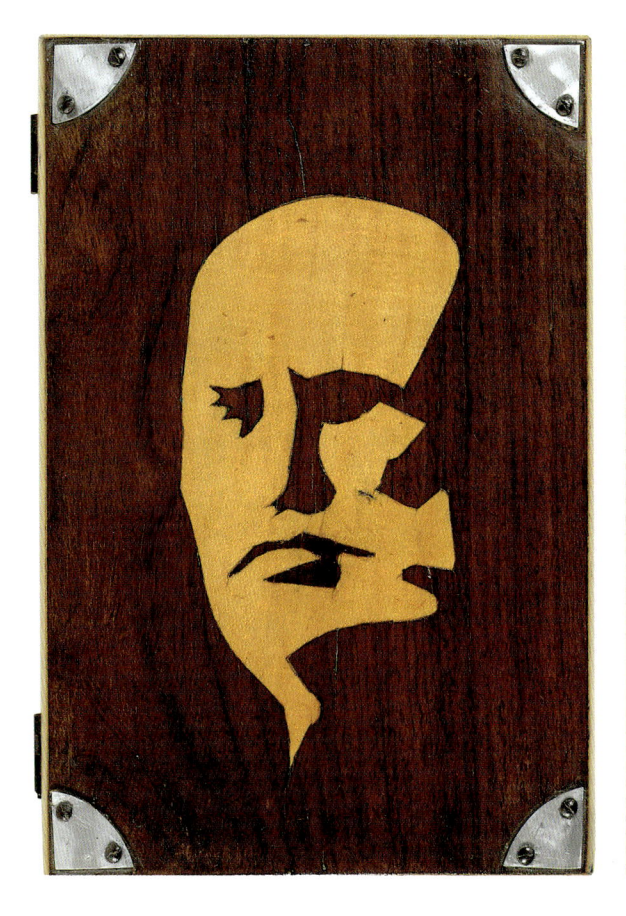

F.F., *His Excellency the Hon. Mussolini*, c. 1926 (cat. no. 84)

Giuseppe Bartoli, *Air Force*, n.d. (1940) (cat. no. 92)

Portrait of Mussolini, c. 1935 (cat. no. 87)

Manzini & Torresani, Verona, *Physico-psychic portrait of the Duce by A.G. Ambrosi*, 1935 (cat. no. 94)

Cornelio Geranzani,
Dux, 1938
(cat. no. 83)

Vela, *Believe Obey Fight*, 1930-35
(cat. no. 97)

Fonderie Fratelli Perani, Brescia, *Lamp*, c. 1935
(cat. no. 98)

Mimì Quilici Buzzacchi, *Study for the fresco in the Chapel dedicated to the Saints Felicita and Perpetua in the Village of Corradini in Libya*, 1940 (cat. no. 101)

Renato Di Bosso, *In Flight above the Colonial Village "M. Bianchi"*, 1938
(cat. no. 100)

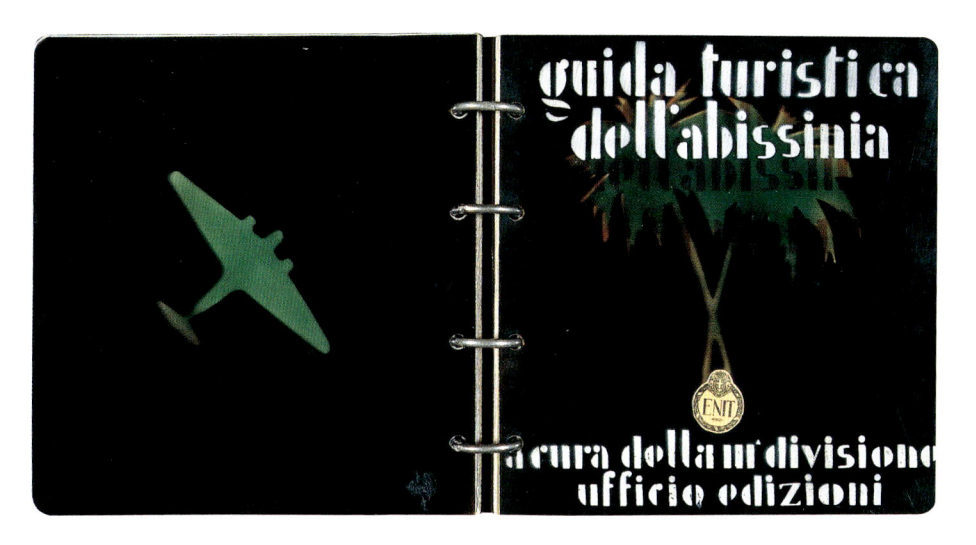

Carlo Vittorio Testi, Ludovico Lambertini,
Guida turistica dell'Abissinia, 1938
(cat. no. 106)

Corrado Mancioli, Ugo Giammusso, *Overseas Triennial Exposition, Naples - 1940 - Year - XVIII*, 1940 (cat. no. 111)

Golia, *Goodbye to Peace*, 1937
(cat. no. 96)

Mario Caffaro Rore, *The Diesel Train on the Sulcis Railway*, 1935
(cat. no. 114)

Fiat, Turin, *Fiat Series II Diesel Train*, 1938
(cat. no. 115)

Giovanni Korompay, *Aeropainting*, 1936
(cat. no. 116)

Alba Giuppone, *Aeropainting - Skimming Flight*,
c. 1942
(cat. no. 118)

Gerardo Dottori, *An Italian of Mussolini (Aerial Portrait of Mario Carli)*, 1931
(cat. no. 117)

Ernesto Thayaht, *The Great Helmsman*, 1939
(cat. no. 119)

Giandante X, *The Hero*, c. 1924

List of Works

1
Corrado Cagli (Ancona 1910 - Rome 1976)
Dante Baldelli (Città di Castello, Perugia 1904-1953)
Rometti, Umbertide
XXVIII October - Believe Obey Fight - In Silence and Strict Discipline - Combat
XXVIII Ottobre - Credere Obbedire Combattere - In silenzio e dura disciplina - Combattimento, 1931-32
4 ceramic tiles, 20 × 20 cm each
GX1993.366-367-368-369

2
La Marcia su Roma, Il Popolo d'Italia, Milan, 1928
GL1997.4.95

3
Francesco Sapori, *L'arte e il Duce*, A. Mondadori, Milan, 1932
GL1993.2.108

4
Giuseppe Bottai, *Politica fascista delle arti*, A. Signorelli Editore, Rome, 1940
cover by Garrasi
GL1993.2.298

5
Dino Alfieri, Luigi Freddi, *Guida della Mostra della Rivoluzione Fascista*, Stabilimenti Grafici A. Vallecchi, Florence, 1932
cover by Mario Sironi (Tempio Pausania, Sassari 1885 - Milan 1961)
GF1993.1.260

6
Dino Alfieri, Luigi Freddi, *Mostra della Rivoluzione Fascista*, Istituto Italiano d'Arti Grafiche, Bergamo, 1933
cover by Mario Sironi (Tempio Pausania, Sassari 1885 - Milan 1961)
GF1993.1.310

7
Marcello Dudovich (Trieste 1878 - Milan 1962)
Roman Salute
Saluto romano, 1925
charcoal on paper, 31.3 × 50 cm
GD1990.482

8
Marcello Dudovich (Trieste 1878 - Milan 1962)
Edizioni STAR, Milan
For Italy in the Name of the Dead!
Per l'Italia nel nome dei morti!, 1924
poster, 137 × 49.5 cm
GX1989.72

9
Filiberto Scarpelli (Naples 1870 - Rome 1933)
Stab. Lit. E. Guazzoni, Rome
Italy Abroad
L'Italia all'estero, 1924
poster, 100 × 140 cm
87.939.4.1

10
Filiberto Scarpelli (Naples 1870 - Rome 1933)
Stab. Lit. E. Guazzoni, Rome
The Lira
La lira, 1924
poster, 100 × 140 cm
87.940.4.1

11
Paolo Troubetzkoy (Intra, Novara 1866 - Suna, Novara 1938)
Benito Mussolini, 1926
bronze, 47 × 18 × 22 cm
GX1993.225

12
Leonetto Cappiello (Livorno 1875 - Cannes 1942)
Stab. Graf. Gros Monti & C., Turin
National Competition for the Victory of Grain
Concorso nazionale per la vittoria del grano, 1926
poster, 140 × 100 cm
GX1993.539.1

13
Cesare Andreoni (Milan 1903-1961)
The Battle for Grain
La battaglia del grano, c. 1935
oil on board, 90 × 80 cm
GX1993.483

14
Domenico Rambelli (Pieve di Ponte, Ravenna 1886 - Rome 1972)
Regia Scuola Ceramica, Faenza
Agricultural Work
Lavoro agricolo, 1926
ceramic panel, 48 × 34 × 3 cm
GX1993.402

15
Melchiorre Melis (Bosa, Nuoro 1889 - Rome 1982)
SCIC, Cagliari
Sardinian Smile
Sorriso di Sardegna, 1929
ceramic plate, Ø 36.3 cm
GD1990.528.1

16
Dino Martens (Venice 1894-1970)
Salviati & C., Venice
Vase, c. 1932
painted glass, 30 × 21.5 cm
GX1993.386

17
Lino Berzoini (Ficarolo, Rovigo 1893 - Albisola Capo, Savona 1971)
Casa Giuseppe Mazzotti, Albisola
Cherish Bread, the Sweet Smell of the Table
Amate il pane profumo della mensa, 1935-38
ceramic plate, Ø 28.5 cm
GD1990.548.1

18
Duilio Cambellotti (Rome 1876-1960)
Fedro Guerrieri, Rome
The Curious Ones
Le curiose, 1923
cabinet, walnut with bronze details, 71 × 96.5 × 47.5 cm
GX1993.208

19
Duilio Cambellotti (Rome 1876-1960)
Night
La notte, 1925
cabinet, walnut with ebony and ivory details, 54 × 80 × 40 cm
GX1993.209

20
Vittorio Grassi (Rome 1878-1958)
FIM (Fabbrica Italiana Mobili, Rome)
Seat, 1923
wood and fabric, 83 × 65 × 65 cm
GD1994.67

21
Vittorio Zecchin (Murano, Venice 1878 - Venice 1947)
Armchair, 1923
black lacquered oak with gilt inlay, 70 × 57.5 × 44 cm
GX1993.48

22
Duilio Cambellotti (Rome 1876-1960)
Nightlight with owls
Veilleuse delle civette, 1924
majolica, 28 × 20 cm
GX1993.113.8

23
Giulio Rufa (Rome 1903 - Milan 1970)
Vase with octopus
Vaso con polpi, 1922
glazed terracotta, 38.5 × 25 cm
GX1993.400

24
Giò Ponti (Milan 1891-1979)
Vintage
Vendemmia, c. 1929
2 ceramic vases, 24 × 19.5 × 15.5 cm each
GX1993.666.1-2
The Mitchell Wolfson Jr. Private Collection

25
La Salamandra, Perugia
Vase, 1930
ceramic, 50 × 32 cm
GX1993.384

26
Ivos Pacetti (Figline di Prato, Florence 1901 - Albisola, Savona 1970)
ILSA, Albisola Capo
Tea service, 1929
ceramic, various dimensions
GD2000.220.1-4
The Mitchell Wolfson Jr. Private Collection

27
Salviati & Co., Venice (attributed to)
Reconciliation between the Church and the Italian State: 11-2-29-A.VII
Riconciliazione tra la Chiesa e lo Stato Italiano: 11-2-29-A.VII, 1929
gilded glass and enamel vase, 19.3 × 23.8 cm
GD1996.169

28
Galileo Chini (Florence 1873-1956)
Chini e Co., Borgo San Lorenzo
Iustitia et pax osculantae sunt, 1929
ceramic plate, h. 6.5 × Ø 30.5 cm
GX1989.53

29
Galileo Chini (Florence 1873-1956)
Chini e Co., Borgo San Lorenzo
Iustitia et pax osculantae sunt, 1929
ceramic plate, h. 6.5 × Ø 28.5 cm
GX1989.54

30
Nico Edel (Aarau, Basel 1901 - Turin 1971)
Gros-Monti & C., Turin
Vercelli and its Province from Romanità to Fascism
Vercelli e la sua provincia dalla romanità al fascismo, 1939
poster, 138.5 × 100 cm
GD1995.116.1

31
Aldo Buttini (Monti di Licciana, Massa Carrara 1898 - Carrara 1957)
Young Boy with Scroll
Fanciullo con cartiglio, c. 1933
bronze, 54 × 25 × 18 cm
GX1993.236

32
Eugenio Baroni (Taranto 1880 - Genoa 1935)
The Sail
La vela, c. 1933
bronze, 56 × 20 × 18 cm
87.1074.6.1

33
Mario Palanti (Milan 1885-1978)
Study for "The Sarcophagus of the Martyrs" in the Chapel of the Fallen, Palazzo del Littorio, Rome
Bozzetto per il "Sarcofago dei Martiri" nella Cappella dei caduti, Palazzo del Littorio, Roma, 1934
bronze and marble, 39 × 52 × 20 cm
GX1993.214

34
Antonio Berti (San Pietro a Sieve, Florence 1904 - Sesto Fiorentino, Florence 1990)
Fonderia Marinelli, Florence
Portrait of Paola Ojetti
Ritratto di Paola Ojetti, 1935
bronze, 68 × 48 × 35 cm
GX1993.212
The Mitchell Wolfson Jr. Private Collection

35
Adolfo De Carolis (Montefiore dell'Aso, Ascoli Piceno 1874 - Rome 1928)
Working in the Mines. Study for the friezes in the Hall of the Provincial Council of Arezzo
Il lavoro delle miniere. Studio per i fregi della sala del Consiglio provinciale di Arezzo, 1922
oil on canvas, 25 × 130 cm
GX1993.441

36
Adolfo De Carolis (Montefiore dell'Aso, Ascoli Piceno 1874 - Rome 1928)
Working in the Fields. Study for the friezes in the Hall of the Provincial Council of Arezzo
Il lavoro dei campi. Studio per i fregi della sala del Consiglio provinciale di Arezzo, 1922
oil on canvas, 25 × 130 cm
GX1993.442

37
Antonio Giuseppe Santagata (Genoa 1888-1985)
The Offering of the Casa Madre to Victory. Study for the fresco in the apse of the Assembly Hall of the Casa Madre dei Mutilati di Guerra in Rome
L'offerta della Casa Madre alla Vittoria. Studio per l'affresco dell'abside del Salone delle Adunate nella Casa Madre dei Mutilati di Guerra a Roma, 1926-32
oil and tempera on paper, 32 × 48.5 cm
87.1063.5.1

38
Antonio Giuseppe Santagata (Genoa 1888-1985)
The Offering of the Casa Madre to Victory. Study for the fresco in the apse of the Assembly Hall of the Casa Madre dei Mutilati di Guerra in Rome
L'offerta della Casa Madre alla Vittoria. Studio per l'affresco dell'abside del Salone delle Adunate nella Casa Madre dei Mutilati di Guerra a Roma, 1926-32
oil, tempera and pencil on paper, 32.7 × 50 cm
87.1064.5.1

39
Duilio Cambellotti (Rome 1876-1960)
Washerwomen. Study for decorations in the Palazzo dell'Acquedotto Pugliese in Bari
Lavandaie. Studio per decorazioni nel Palazzo dell'Acquedotto Pugliese a Bari, 1931
tempera on heliograph on card, 48 × 94.5 cm
GX1993.113.28.29

40
Italo Balbo's Crossing. Studies for decorations in the Ministry of Aeronautics in Rome, c. 1931
pencil and pastel on card, 39 × 39 cm each
GX1993.470.1-6

41
Duilio Cambellotti (Rome 1876-1960)
Triptych of the Victory. Study for decorations in the Palazzo del Governo in Ragusa
Trittico della Vittoria. Studio per decorazioni nel Palazzo del Governo di Ragusa, 1933
tempera on heliograph on plywood, 81.9 × 97.6 cm
GX1993.113.19.126

42
Alberto Salietti (Ravenna 1892 - Chiavari, Genoa 1961)
The Empire. Study for the competition "Mosaic decoration in the Hall of the Palace of Receptions and Conferences", E42, Rome
L'Impero. Bozzetto per il concorso "La decorazione in mosaico nel Salone del Palazzo dei ricevimenti e congressi" all'E42 a Roma, 1940-41
tempera on paper, 32.9 × 66 cm
GD2002.254.2

43
Alberto Salietti (Ravenna 1892 - Chiavari, Genoa 1961)
Mussolini's Rome. Study for the competition "Mosaic decoration in the Hall of the Palace of Receptions and Conferences", E42, Rome
Roma di Mussolini. Bozzetto per il concorso "La decorazione in mosaico nel Salone del Palazzo dei ricevimenti e congressi" all'E42 a Roma, 1940-41
tempera on paper, 32.9 × 66 cm
GD2002.254.4

44
Galileo Chini (Florence 1873-1956)
Construction Work
Il lavoro edilizio, c. 1935
mixed media on paper, 127 × 68 cm
GX1993.510

45
Galileo Chini (Florence 1873-1956)
Steelworks
Il lavoro delle acciaierie, c. 1935
mixed media on paper, 127.5 × 68.5 cm
GX1993.511

46
Giuseppe Pagano (Parenzo, Istria 1896 - Mauthausen 1945)
Gino Levi Montalcini (Milan 1902 - Turin 1974)
FIP (Fabbrica Italiana Pianoforti), Turin
Armchair for the Gualino Offices in Turin, 1928
buxus, 67 × 53 × 48 cm
GX1993.204

47
Marcello Piacentini (Rome 1881-1960)
Seat for the entrance hall of Fiammetta Sarfatti's house in Rome, 1933
firwood and plywood, 90 × 43 × 42.3 cm
GD1993.5.1

48
Marcello Piacentini (Rome 1881-1960)
Seat for the entrance hall of Fiammetta Sarfatti's house in Rome, 1933
firwood and plywood, h. 90 × Ø 44 cm
GD1993.6.1

49
Luigi Vietti (Novara 1903 - Milan 1998)
Armchair for the Andrea Doria maritime station in Genoa, 1933
laminated walnut, 72 × 60 × 66 cm
GG1998.1
Gift of Autorità Portuale Genoa

50
Primo Sinopico (Raoul Chareun, Cagliari 1889 - Milan 1949)
SPICA, Albisola
Plate with skyscrapers and aeroplane, c. 1930
ceramic, Ø 40.5 cm
GD1996.171

51
Romeo Bevilacqua (Florence 1908 - Savona 1958)
Casa Giuseppe Mazzotti, Albisola
Game of Billiards
Partita a biliardo, 1932-34
ceramic plate, Ø 37 cm
87.942.7.1

52
Romeo Bevilacqua (Florence 1908 - Savona 1958)
Casa Giuseppe Mazzotti, Albisola
Motorcyclists
Motociclisti, 1932-34
ceramic plate, Ø 37 cm
87.943.7.1

53
Nicolaj Diulgheroff (Kiustendil, Bulgaria 1901 - Turin 1982)
Casa Giuseppe Mazzotti, Albisola
Vase, c. 1932
ceramic, 41 × 41 cm
87.941.7.1

54
Ivos Pacetti (Figline di Prato, Florence 1901 - Albisola, Savona 1970)
La Fiamma, Albisola
Vase, c. 1933
ceramic, 19.5 × 16 cm
GD2000.228.1

55
Guido Andlovitz (Trieste 1900 - Grado, Gorizia 1971)
Società Ceramica Italiana, Laveno
Coffee set, 1933
porcelain, various dimension
GD1994.71.1-17

56
Dante Baldelli (Città di Castello, Perugia 1904-1953)
Rometti, Umbertide
Vase with archers, 1933-34
ceramic, 44 × 26 cm
GX1993.387

57
Ugo Carà (Muggia, Trieste 1908)
Bowl, 1931
chrome-plated metal, h. 9 × Ø 14 cm
GD2002.257
The Mitchell Wolfson Jr. Private Collection

58
Ugo Carà (Muggia, Trieste 1908)
Plant-holder, 1933

chrome-plated metal, 18.5 × 24 cm
GD2002.256
The Mitchell Wolfson Jr. Private Collection

59
Luigi Genazzi, Milan
Centrepiece with plate, c. 1935
silver and ebony, 23 × 27 × 19 cm (centrepiece);
3.5 × 39 × 34 cm (plate)
GX1993.379.1-2

60
Giò Ponti (Milan 1891-1979)
Krupp, Milan
Soup tureen, c. 1936
silver-plated nickel, 22 × 33 cm
GX1989.56a,b

61
Giò Ponti (Milan 1891-1979)
MITA, Genoa Nervi
Carpet design with chairs, 1935
pencil on paper
Archivio MITA-Ponis, Genoa-Rome, on loan to The Mitchell Wolfson Jr. Collection, Genoa

62
Alberto Bevilacqua (Palermo 1896 - Rome 1979)
MITA, Genoa Nervi
Study for the "Wrestlers" carpet
Bozzetto per tappeto "Lottatori", 1929
tempera on paper, 29.8 × 36.5 cm
Archivio MITA-Ponis, Genoa-Rome, on loan to The Mitchell Wolfson Jr. Collection, Genoa

63
Emanuele Rambaldi (Pieve di Teco, Imperia 1903 - Savona 1968)
MITA, Genoa Nervi
Carpet design, n.d.
tempera on paper,
34 × 46 cm
Archivio MITA-Ponis, Genoa-Rome, on loan to The Mitchell Wolfson Jr. Collection, Genoa

64
Fortunato Depero (Fondo, Trento 1892 - Rovereto, Trento 1960)
MITA, Genoa Nervi
Carpet design, 1927
collage, 40 × 50 cm
GM2000.57.3
Archivio MITA-Ponis, Genoa-Rome, on loan to The Mitchell Wolfson Jr. Collection, Genoa

65
Erberto Carboni (Parma 1899 - Milan 1984)
Boschi Luigi & Sons
Boschi Luigi & Figli, 1926
playbill, 33.3 × 23 cm
GD1996.191

66
Alf Gaudenzi (Genoa 1908-1980)
The Waiter
Il cameriere, 1933
design for an advertisement, mixed media on card, 31 × 20.5 cm
GG2000.16.1
Gift of Ambra Gaudenzi, Genoa

67
Atla (Giovanni Mingozzi, Bologna 1891-?)
Barbisio Handmade Hat
Barbisio-Cappello lavorato a mano, 1933
playbill, 23.7 × 16.5 cm
GD1990.554

68
Atla (Giovanni Mingozzi, Bologna 1891-?)
Verelyte: "The Great Headscarf". Barbisio
Verelyte: "Il gran foulard". Barbisio, 1933
playbill, 18.7 × 21 cm
GD1990.555

69
Sepo (Severo Pozzati, Comacchio, Ferrara 1895 - Bologna 1983)
Noveltex! Evening
Noveltex! Soir, 1936
playbill, 38.7 × 20.5 cm
GX1993.634.1

70
Sepo (Severo Pozzati, Comacchio, Ferrara 1895 - Bologna 1983)
Noveltex Sport, 1936
playbill, 28.7 × 13.2 cm
GX1993.635.1

71
Giovanni Mingozzi (Bologna 1891 - ?)
Barbisio, 1936
playbill, 31.2 × 20.7 cm
GD1990.484

72
Huge Reductions Lama Italia
Grandi ribassi Lama Italia, 1941
playbill, 17 × 47.6 cm
GX1993.633.1

73
Tullio D'Albisola (Albisola, Savona 1899-1971)
Bruno Munari (Milan 1907-1998)
Edizioni Futuriste di "Poesia," Rome; Litolatta, Savona
L'anguria lirica, 1934
lithograph on tin
GF1993.1.25

74
Ubaldo Cosimo Veneziani (Bologna 1894 - Milan 1958)
Portrait of a Mother and Child
Ritratto di madre con il figlio, c. 1935
oil on canvas, 121 × 100 cm
GX1993.516

75
Verossì (Albino Siviero, Verona 1904 - Cerro Veronese, Verona 1945)
Balilla, 1937
oil on board, 108 × 84 cm
GD1994.86.1

76
Guido Galletti (London 1893 - Genoa 1977)
Boy Throwing a Stone (Balilla)
Ragazzo che scaglia una pietra (Balilla), 1931
bronze, 123 × 54 × 27 cm
GX1993.215

77
Antonio (Tony) Lucarda (Vicenza 1904 - Venice 1992)
Balilla Drummer-Boy
Balilla tamburino, 1934
plaster, 88 × 42 × 46 cm
GG1995.2.1
Gift of Marjorie Lucarda, Venice

78
Bot (Barbieri Oswaldo Terribile, Piacenza 1895-1958)
Opera Balilla Grade I Diploma
Opera Balilla Diploma di I Grado, 1934
diploma, 30 × 50 cm
87.881.19.1

79
Mario Sironi (Tempio Pausania, Sassari 1885 - Milan 1961)
The Soldier and the Worker
Il soldato e il lavoratore, 1943
tempera on card, 38 × 30.5 cm
GX1993.520

80
Gino Boccasile (Bari 1901 - Milan 1952)
25 July
25 luglio, 1943
tempera on card, 68.5 × 48.5 cm
GX1993.51

81
Valenti
These are the Liberators
Questi sono i liberatori, c. 1943
charcoal and coloured crayon on paper,
47.2 × 35.2 cm
GX1993.537

82
Giorgio Matteo Aicardi (Finalborgo, Savona 1891 - Genoa 1985)
Duce. Studies for the fresco on a building façade in Busalla on the occasion of the visit of Mussolini to Genoa, May 1938
Duce. Studi per l'affresco di una facciata di edificio a Busalla in occasione della visita di Mussolini a Genova, Maggio 1938, 1938
mixed media on paper on card,
51.7 × 23.6 cm
GG2002.30

83
Cornelio Geranzani (Genoa 1880-1955)
Dux, 1938
panel, inlaid wood, 80 × 61.7 cm
GD2002.253
The Mitchell Wolfson Jr. Private Collection

84
F.F.
His Excellency the Hon. Mussolini
Sua Eccellenza Onorevole Mussolini,
c. 1926
ceramic plate, Ø 24 cm
GD1993.10.1

85
Renato Bertelli (Lastra a Signa, Florence 1900-1974)
Officine Scudo, Milan
Continuous Profile of Mussolini
Profilo continuo di Mussolini, 1933
paperweight, brass and bakelite, 9.5 × 7 cm
GD1990.444.1

86
SMI, Florence
Mussolini and Victor Emmanuel III, 1939
paperweight, iron and brass,
19.5 × 10.5 × 2.3 cm
87.853.6.1

87
Portrait of Mussolini, c. 1935
box, inlaid wood, 25.5 × 8.5 × 6.5 cm
GX1993.362

88
Aurelio Mistruzzi (Villaorba di Basiliano, Udine 1880 - Rome 1960)

Stabilimento A. Staderini, Rome
P.N.F. (Partito Nazionale Fascista) Fascist Calendar 1929
P.N.F. Calendario fascista 1929, 1928
calendar, 37.3 × 28 cm
GE1995.3.2

89
Istituto Italiano d'Arti Grafiche, Bergamo
P.N.F. (Partito Nazionale Fascista) Fascist Calendar Year IX-MCMXXXI
P.N.F. Calendario fascista A. IX-MCMXXXI,
1930
calendar, 33.7 × 23.5 cm
GE1993.2.311

90
Aeropoeti aeropittori di guerra. Gruppo futurista Savarè, VIII Mostra di aeropitture di guerra, Padua, 1940
GF1993.1.33

91
Luccio (Carlo Bolognesi)
Edizione Propaganda Nazionale Casamorati, Bologna
Italian Products
Prodotti italiani, c. 1922
postcard, 9 × 14.1 cm
GE1993.1.173

92
Giuseppe Bartoli
Rag. F. Duval Editore, Milan
Air Force
Arma aeronautica, n.d. (1940)
postcard, 10.6 × 14.9 cm
GE1993.1.184

93
G. Giannini, Florence
Dux: Plastic synthesis in steel by Ernesto Thayaht
Dux: sintesi plastica in acciaio di Ernesto Thayaht, 1929
postcard, 14.4 × 9.3 cm
GE1994.2.232

94
Manzini & Torresani, Verona
Physico-psychic Portrait of the Duce by A.G. Ambrosi
Ritratto fisico-psichico del Duce di A.G. Ambrosi, 1935
postcard, 14.2 × 9.4 cm
GE1994.2.236

95
Ernesto (Michahelles) Thayaht (Florence 1893 - Pietrasanta, Lucca 1959)

Rome Year X. First Meeting of Professionals and Artists
Roma Anno Decimo. Prima adunata professionisti e artisti, 1932
silver medal, Ø 5 cm
GD1990.437

96
Golia (Eugenio Colmo, Turin 1885 - 1967)
Lenci, Turin
Goodbye to Peace
Addio alla pace, 1937
ceramic bowl, h. 8 × Ø 30 cm
GD2001.244
The Mitchell Wolfson Jr. Private Collection

97
Vela
Believe Obey Fight
Credere Obbedire Combattere, 1930-35
clock, wood and chrome-plated metal,
31 × 29 × 6.5 cm
GX1993.304

98
Fonderie Fratelli Perani, Brescia
Lamp, c. 1935
bronze with marble base, 60 × 17 × 31 cm
GD1994.73.1

99
Fasces lamp, c. 1935
metal, 106 × 39 × 12 cm
GD1995.119.1

100
Renato Di Bosso (Renato Righetti, Verona 1905 - Arbizzano di Valpolicella, Verona 1982)
In Flight above the Colonial Village "M. Bianchi"
In volo sul villaggio coloniale "M. Bianchi",
1938
oil on masonite, 89.5 × 100 cm
87.1070.5.1

101
Mimì Quilici Buzzacchi (Medole, Mantua 1903 - Rome 1990)
Study for the fresco in the Chapel dedicated to the Saints Felicita and Perpetua in the Village of Corradini in Libya
Studio per l'affresco nella Cappella dedicata alle Sante Felicita e Perpetua nel villaggio Corradini in Libia, 1940
oil on plywood, 100 × 61 cm
GX1993.468

102
Tripoli 1933 Catalogo, Ente Autonomo Fiera

di Tripoli, Istituto Geografico De Agostini,
Novara, 1933
GL1993.2.305

103
X Fiera di Tripoli, Ente Autonomo Fiera
di Tripoli, Arti Grafiche Bertarelli, Milan-
Rome, 1935
cover by Giuseppe Casolaro
GL1997.4.519

104
XI Fiera di Tripoli, Ente Autonomo Fiera
di Tripoli, Istituto Geografico De Agostini,
Novara, 1936
cover by Carlo Vittorio Testi (Ravina, Trento
1902)
GL1997.4.520

105
Vademecum per l'A.O., Bompiani, Milan, 1936
GL1993.2.98

106
Carlo Vittorio Testi (Ravina, Trento 1902)
Ludovico Lambertini (Bologna 1876-1959)
ENIT
Guida turistica dell'Abissinia, 1938
mixed media on plastic and card, 16 × 15 cm
GF1993.1.340

107
Santagostino, Milan
Stabilimento Grafico Ripalta, Milan
*The Ethiopian War and the Santagostino
Super-Race*
*La guerra d'Etiopia e la super-gara
Santagostino*, 1936
game, 50.5 × 70.5 cm
GE2001.3.258

108
Ditta A. Sutter, Genoa
Officine dell'Istituto Italiano d'Arti Grafiche,
Bergamo
The Economic Conquest of the Empire
Alla conquista economica dell'Impero, 1937
game, 55.5 × 41 cm
GE1994.2.212

109
The Italian Empire
Impero italiano, c. 1938
album, leather and metal, 41.5 × 31 cm
87.889.16.1

110
Società Ceramica Italiana, Laveno
*The Ignazio Messina & Co. Postal Line
for the Ethiopian Empire*
*Linea postale per l'Impero Etiopico Ignazio
Messina & C.*, c. 1935
porcelain ashtray, 10.5 × 13 × 2 cm
GX1993.358

111
Corrado Mancioli (Rome 1904-1958), Ugo
Giammusso (Caltanissetta 1908 - Rome 1977)
SPICA, Albisola
*Overseas Triennial Exposition, Naples - 1940 -
Year XVIII*
Triennale d'Oltremare, Napoli - 1940 - XVIII,
1940
ceramic panel, 23.6 × 16.7 × 5.5 cm
GD1990.574.1

112
Tip. E. Padoan, Milan
Triennale d'Oltremare. Guida mobile ufficiale,
1940
cover by Corrado Mancioli (Rome 1904-1958)
GE1993.2.225

113
Dario Cella
Stab. Tip. F. Raimondi, Naples
*Publicity at the First Triennial Exposition
of Italian overseas territories*
*La pubblicità alla Prima Mostra Triennale
delle terre italiane d'oltremare*, 1939
series of postcards, 15 × 10.5 cm each
GE1993.2.224.1-3

114
Mario Caffaro Rore (Turin 1910)
Gros Monti & C., Turin
The Diesel Train on the Sulcis Railway
La littorina sulla ferrovia del Sulcis, 1935
poster, 100 × 66.3 cm
GD1993.2.1

115
Fiat, Turin
Fiat Series II Diesel Train
Littorina Fiat II serie mod. 1938, 1938
model, aluminium, leather and wood,
32 × 166 × 28 cm
GX1993.203

116
Giovanni Korompay (Venice 1904 -
Rovereto, Trento 1988)
Aeropainting
Aeropittura, 1936
oil on plywood, 120 × 132 cm
GX1993.497

117
Gerardo Dottori (Perugia 1884-1977)
*An Italian of Mussolini (Aerial Portrait
of Mario Carli)*
*Un italiano di Mussolini (Ritratto aereo
di Mario Carli)*, 1931
oil on canvas, 159 × 129.5 cm
GX1993.462

118
Alba Giuppone (Berne 1902 - Chivasso,
Turin 1978)
Aeropainting - Skimming Flight
Aeropittura - Volo radente, c. 1942
oil on plywood, 109 × 131 cm
GX1993.484

119
Ernesto (Michahelles) Thayaht (Florence
1893 - Pietrasanta, Lucca 1959)
The Great Helmsman
Il grande nocchiere, 1939
oil on canvas, 161 × 98.5 cm
GD1993.7.1

Finito di stampare nel settembre 2002
presso le Arti Grafiche Salea di Milano
per conto delle Edizioni Gabriele Mazzotta